MENSA
THE MIND OBSTACLE COURSE

THIS IS A CARLTON BOOK
This edition produced for Book Sales, Inc.

Text and puzzle content copyright © British Mensa Limited 1998
Design and artwork copyright © Carlton Books Limited 1998

This book is sold subject to the conditions that it shall not, by way of trade or otherwise, be lent, resold, hired out or otherwise circulated without the publisher's prior written consent in any form of cover or binding other than that in which it is published and without a similar condition including this condition, being imposed upon the subsequent purchaser.

All rights reserved.

ISBN 0-78580-955 4

Printed and bound in Italy

MENSA
THE MIND OBSTACLE COURSE

Dave Chatten and Carolyn Skitt

CHARTWELL BOOKS, INC.

AMERICAN MENSA LTD

American Mensa Ltd is an organization for individuals who have one common trait: an IQ in the top 2% in the nation. Over 50,000 current members have found out how smart they are. This leaves room for an additional 4.5 million members in America alone. You may be one of them.

Looking for intellectual stimulation?

If you enjoy mental exercise, you'll find lots of good "workout programs" in the *Mensa Bulletin*, our national magazine. Voice your opinion in one of the newsletters published by each of our 150 local chapters. Learn from the many books and publications that are available to you as a member.

Looking for social interaction?

Are you a "people person," or would you like to meet other people with whom you feel comfortable? Then come to our local meetings, parties, and get-togethers. Participate in our lectures and debates. Attend our regional events and national gatherings. There's something happening on the Mensa calendar almost daily. So, you have lots of opportunities to meet people, exchange ideas, and make interesting new friends.

Looking for others who share your special interest?

Whether yours is as common as crossword puzzles or as esoteric as Egyptology, there's a Mensa Special Interest Group (SIG) for it.

Take the challenge. Find out how smart you really are. Mensans love to read so already have something in common.

Contact American Mensa Ltd today and ask for a free brochure. We enjoy adding new members and ideas to our high-IQ organization.

American Mensa Ltd
201 Main Street, Suite 1101
Fort Worth, Texas 76102

or, if you don't live in the USA:

Mensa International
15 The Ivories
628 Northampton Street
London N1 2NY
England   will be happy to put you in touch with your own national Mensa

CONTENTS

ZONE 1
- The Deduction Crawl 6
- **The Mensa Mind Obstacle Course Scoring System 21**
- Answers 22
- Scoring System 30

ZONE 2
- The Number Jump 31
- Answers 60
- Scoring System 67

ZONE 3
- The Word Climb 68
- Answers 72
- Scoring System 75

ZONE 4
- The Memory Tests 76
- Answers 104
- Scoring System 106

ZONE 5
- The Spatial Logic Dodge 107
- Answers 127
- Scoring System 128

On your mark...

Get set...

GO..!

ZONE 1

Find your way to the end of 238 riddles requiring deductive powers worthy of Sherlock Holmes.

OBSTACLE 1 What letter appears once only in each of the first two words but not at all in the last two words?

1.	FRUITAGE	INTERPLAY	but not in	INTERMISSION	OSTEOPOROSIS
2.	RIPCORD	SHIELDING	but not in	WISTFUL	OCTAGONAL
3.	PINNACLE	COMPLAISANT	but not in	PINCERS	MATCHBOX
4.	IMPLICATION	MULTIFORD	but not in	STAMINA	WARDSHIP
5.	YEOMANLY	VALENCE	but not in	SPADEWORK	CARAMELIZE
6.	RAMSHACKLE	MARSHMALLOW	but not in	STARDUST	OCCUPATION
7.	PAWNBROKER	SINKAGE	but not in	WONDERFUL	SACRIFICE
8.	WINDSCREEN	IMPARTIAL	but not in	FICTITIOUS	CAMPAIGN
9.	INCRIMINATE	FINGERPRINT	but not in	ALPINE	BLUEBELL
10.	COBBLESTONE	ESTIMATE	but not in	GRANITE	IGNORANCE
11.	JAVELIN	ABRASIVE	but not in	PROMPTITUDE	RHOMBUS
12.	PICTURESQUE	IMMACULATE	but not in	SITUATION	HIDEOUS
13.	EDUCATIONAL	MUNDANE	but not in	STEADILY	RIDGEPOLE
14.	RICOCHET	GEOLOGICAL	but not in	OSPREY	POLYCARBON
15.	ROBUSTIOUS	SPELLBOUND	but not in	THUNDERCLAP	MOUTHPIECE
16.	LYRICISM	HAMSTRING	but not in	THISTLEDOWN	WORDLESS
17.	SORTILEGE	DISGRACED	but not in	PRIESTHOOD	SOPRANO
18.	GRAPEFRUIT	ACIDIFIES	but not in	HEADLAND	INVENTIVE
19.	SPECIFY	INVARIABLE	but not in	LAMINATION	STANDARD
20.	AROMATHERAPY	INSPECTION	but not in	MAGNIFICENT	DIRECTOR

Answers on page 22

ZONE 1

THE DEDUCTION CRAWL

OBSTACLE 2 Remove one letter from the first word and place it into the second word to form two new words. You must not change the order of the letters in the words and you may not use plurals. What letter needs to move?

21.	SALLOW	BAIL
22.	PITCH	SALE
23.	PRIDE	SLOE
24.	SWAMP	CLAP
25.	STILL	FACE
26.	THREE	NICE
27.	VALUE	CASE
28.	WHEAT	FAST
29.	MONTH	GLAD
30.	METAL	HOLY
31.	WRING	FIST
32.	TWINE	COME
33.	PROUD	BOND
34.	DARTED	BEACH
35.	CURVED	SHOE
36.	CREASE	BAND
37.	BUNGLE	CATER
38.	BRIDGE	FINER
39.	TWAIN	HUNT
40.	STOOP	FLAT

OBSTACLE 3 What word has a similar meaning to the first word and rhymes with the second word?

41.	CRACK	—	DRAKE
42.	BOTTOM	—	CASE
43.	RELAX	—	BEST
44.	TRUMPET	—	CUBA
45.	TRUE	—	MEAL
46.	REAR	—	LACK
47.	HOOP	—	SING
48.	CORROSION	—	MUST
49.	GRIT	—	HAND
50.	THREAD	—	GRAND

Answers on page 22

ZONE 1

OBSTACLE 4 Look at the shape below and answer the following questions on it.

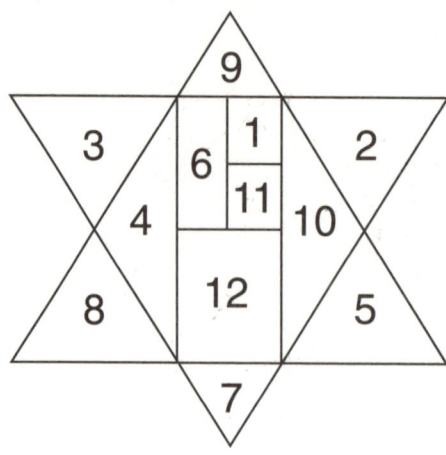

51. How many triangles are there in the diagram?
52. How many rectangles are there in the diagram?
53. How many hexagons can you find?
54. Deduct the sum of the numbers in the rectangles from the sum of the numbers in the triangles.

OBSTACLE 5 In the supermarket, the aisles are numbered one to six from the entrance. Washing powder is next to bottles and it is not the first item you see when entering the supermarket. You will see the meat aisle before the bread aisle. Tins are two aisles before bottles and meat is four aisles after fruit.

55. What is in the last aisle (aisle six)?
56. In which aisle can bottles be found?
57. What is in the first aisle?
58. In which aisle can tins be found?

ZONE 1

OBSTACLE 6 In a car showroom, the white car is at one end of the showroom and the purple car is at the other. The red car is next to the black car and three places away from the blue car. The yellow car is next to the blue car and nearer to the purple car than to the white one. The silver car is next to the red one and the green car is five places away from the blue car. The black car is next to the green car.

59. Is the silver car or the red car nearer to the purple car?
60. Which car is three places away from the white car?
61. Which car is next to the purple car?
62. Which car is between the silver and the blue?

OBSTACLE 7 A survey has been conducted on the types of holidays people have taken over the last twelve months. Five more people had one holiday only and stayed in a self-catering accommodation than had one holiday and stayed in a hotel. Eight people had a camping holiday only and five people took all three types of holiday. Fifty-nine people had not stayed in a hotel in the last twelve months. Four times as many people went camping only as had a hotel and a camping holiday but no self-catering holiday. Of the 107 who took part in the survey a total of 35 people took a camping holiday.

63. How many people only had a hotel holiday?
64. How many people stayed in self-catering accommodation and a hotel but did not camp?
65. How many people did not stay in self-catering accommodation?
66. How many people stayed in only two of the three types of accommodation?

OBSTACLE 8 In a day at the library, 64 people borrowed books. Twice as many people borrowed a thriller only as borrowed a science fiction only. Three people borrowed a biography only and 11 people borrowed both science fiction and a thriller but not a biography. The same number borrowed a biography and a thriller but no science fiction as borrowed one of each of the three types. Twenty-one people did not borrow a thriller. One more person borrowed a science fiction book and a biography book than borrowed a biography only.

67. How many biographies were borrowed in total?
68. How many people borrowed only two of the three types?
69. How many people borrowed a thriller, a biography and a science fiction?
70. How many people borrowed a thriller only?

Answers on pages 23 & 24

THE DEDUCTION CRAWL

ZONE 1

THE DEDUCTION CRAWL

OBSTACLE 9 — What word, which is alphabetically between the two given words, answers the clues?

71.	CURIOUS	—	CURRANT	Twist or roll
72.	BARRICADE	—	BARROW	Obstruction
73.	CABRIOLET	—	CAMPAIGN	French town famous for cheese
74.	CALM	—	CALVARY	Unit of energy
75.	DAUGHTER	—	DAY	Beginning
76.	DUO	—	DUPLICATE	Deceive
77.	EPIC	—	EPIGRAM	Widespread disease
78.	EPISODE	—	EPITAPH	Letter
79.	FAINT	—	FAITH	Fantasy world
80.	FALSE	—	FAME	Waver
81.	GOLD	—	GONDOLA	A sport
82.	GRAFT	—	GRAMMAR	Cereal
83.	HEROINE	—	HERSELF	Fishbone pattern
84.	HESITATE	—	HEW	Coarse fabric
85.	IMMATURE	—	IMMERSE	Instant
86.	JOG	—	JOKE	Junction of two or more parts
87.	KIOSK	—	KISMET	Smoked fish
88.	LEAF	—	LEAK	An association
89.	LIMBER	—	LIMIT	Rhyme
90.	MEDDLE	—	MEDICAL	Intervene

OBSTACLE 10 — Match the word groups below with the given words.

91. EXTRA
92. WALL
93. VENUS
94. BEND
95. NONE

A	B	C	D	E
Mercury	Zero	Arch	Surplus	Fence
Pluto	Nil	Bow	Excess	Gate
Jupiter	Nought	Curve	Residue	Hedge
Saturn	Nothing	Concave	Remainder	Barrier

Answers on page 24

ZONE 1

THE DEDUCTION CRAWL

OBSTACLE 11 Match the word groups below with the given words.

96. WAYNE
97. FOXGLOVE
98. GARNISH
99. TOUGH
100. TWILIGHT

A	B	C	D	E
Dusk	Brando	Durable	Poppy	Trimmings
Sundown	Bogart	Strong	Crocus	Accessories
Sunset	Travolta	Sturdy	Peony	Frills
Nightfall	Swayze	Hardy	Aster	Extras

OBSTACLE 12 Match the word groups below with the given words.

101. JACKET
102. CONSTABLE
103. PUZZLE
104. CHOPIN
105. CUT

A	B	C	D	E
Ernst	Borodin	Reduce	Baffle	Cover
Rembrandt	Vivaldi	Decrease	Bewilder	Wrapper
Dali	Liszt	Lessen	Confuse	Sleeve
Picasso	Elgar	Curtail	Flummox	Envelope

Answers on pages 24 & 25

ZONE 1

OBSTACLE 13
Match the word groups below with the given words.

106. FRANKENSTEIN
107. COUNTRY
108. ANISEED
109. FEELING
110. TRANQUIL

A	B	C	D	E
Calm	Cumin	Kingdom	Werewolf	Theory
Peaceful	Nutmeg	Realm	Demon	View
Restful	Thyme	State	Dracula	Belief
Serene	Saffron	Nation	Vampire	Opinion

OBSTACLE 14

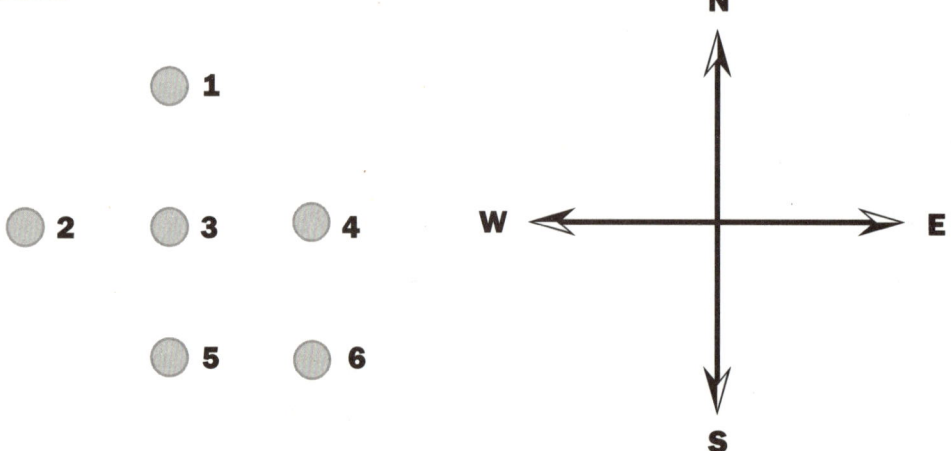

In the map above, C is south of A and south-east of D. B is south-west of F and north-west of E.

111. Which town is at point 1?
112. Which town is furthest west?
113. Which town is south-west of A?
114. Which town is north of D?
115. Which town is at point 6?

ZONE 1

THE DEDUCTION CRAWL

OBSTACLE 15   A certain month has five Wednesdays and the third Saturday is the 18th.

116. How many Mondays are in the month?
117. What is the date of the last Sunday of the month?
118. What is the date of the third Wednesday of the month?
119. On what day does the 23rd fall?
120. On what day does the 7th fall?

OBSTACLE 16   Three cousins have washing pegged out on the line. On each line there is a shirt, a jumper and a towel. Each has one spotted, one plain and one striped item but none of them has the same item in the same design as their cousins. Sandra's jumper is the same design as Paul's towel and Paul's jumper is the same design as Kerry's towel. Kerry's jumper is striped and Sandra's shirt is spotted.

121. Who has a spotted jumper?
122. What design is Sandra's towel?
123. Who has a striped shirt?
124. What design is Kerry's jumper?
125. What design is Paul's towel?

OBSTACLE 17   Three children, Joanna, Richard and Thomas have a pen, a crayon and a pencil-case on their desks. Each has one cat, one elephant and one rabbit design on their item but none has the same item in the same design as the others. Joanna's pencil-case is the same design as Thomas's pen and Richard's pen is the same design as Joanna's crayon. Richard has a cat on his pencil-case and Thomas has an elephant on his pen.

126. Who has a cat on their pen?
127. What design is Richard's crayon?
128. Who has a rabbit on their pencil-case?
129. What design is Thomas's pencil-case?
130. Who has a rabbit on their crayon?

Answers on page 25

ZONE 1

OBSTACLE 18 The numbers on the right are formed from the numbers on the left using the same formula in each question. Find the rule and replace the question mark with a number.

131.
4 → 13
7 → 22
1 → 4
9 → ?

132.
6 → 2
13 → 16
17 → 24
8 → ?

133.
8 → 23
3 → 13
11 → 29
2 → ?

134.
6 → 10
5 → 8
17 → 32
12 → ?

135.
18 → 15
20 → 16
6 → 9
14 → ?

136.
31 → 12
15 → 4
13 → 3
41 → ?

137.
10 → 12
19 → 30
23 → 38
14 → ?

138.
9 → 85
6 → 40
13 → 173
4 → ?

139.
361 → 22
121 → 14
81 → 12
25 → ?

140.
21 → 436
15 → 220
8 → 59
3 → ?

141.
5 → 65
2 → 50
14 → 110
8 → ?

142.
15 → 16
34 → 92
13 → 8
20 → ?

143.
5 → 38
12 → 80
23 → 146
9 → ?

144.
7 → 15
16 → 51
4 → 3
21 → ?

Answers on page 26

ZONE 1

145. 36 → 12
56 → 17
12 → 6
40 → ?

146. 145 → 26
60 → 9
225 → 42
110 → ?

147. 25 → 72
31 → 108
16 → 18
19 → ?

148. 8 → 99
11 → 126
26 → 261
15 → ?

149. 8 → 100
13 → 225
31 → 1089
17 → ?

150. 29 → 5
260 → 16
13 → 3
40 → ?

OBSTACLE 19

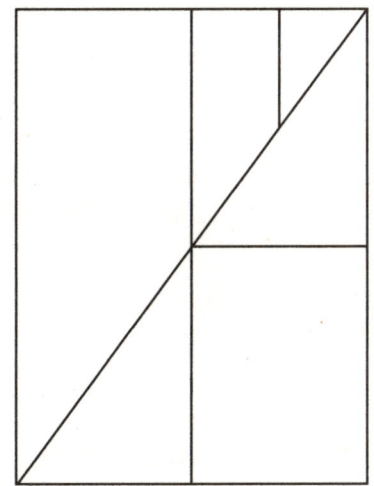

151. How many different sections are there in the drawing?
152. How many triangles are in the drawing?
153. How many rectangles are in the drawing?
154. How many right angles are in the drawing?
155. If the vertical middle line is central, how many similar triangles are there?

THE DEDUCTION CRAWL

ZONE 1

OBSTACLE 20

	MONKEYS	LLAMAS	LIONS
WILDLIFE PARK A	42	25	16
WILDLIFE PARK B	35	21	14
WILDLIFE PARK C	48	32	10

156. Which park has twice as many monkeys as Park B has llamas?
157. Which park has one quarter of the total lions?
158. At which park does the sum of the llamas and lions total the number of monkeys?
159. Which park has three times as many monkeys as Park A has lions?
160. Which park has twice as many llamas as one of the parks has lions?

OBSTACLE 21
Can you find a word that begins with the letter "A", which is opposite in meaning to the given word?

- **161.** VANISH
- **162.** BELOW
- **163.** FORFEIT
- **164.** CONVICT
- **165.** SWEETNESS
- **166.** PRESENT
- **167.** IMAGINARY
- **168.** EXTEND
- **169.** OPPRESSIVE
- **170.** IMMATURE

OBSTACLE 22
Can you find a word beginning with the letter "H", which is opposite in meaning to the following?

- **171.** EXCEPTIONAL
- **172.** SERIOUS
- **173.** DIGNIFY
- **174.** FRIENDLY
- **175.** DOCILE
- **176.** FREE
- **177.** DESPAIRING
- **178.** PROSPERITY
- **179.** VILLAIN
- **180.** SATISFIED

ZONE 1

OBSTACLE 23 In a picture showing a winter scene there are people wearing hats, scarves and gloves. The same number can be seen wearing a hat only as wearing a scarf and gloves only. There are only four people who are not wearing a hat. Five people are wearing a hat and a scarf but no gloves. Twice as many people are wearing a hat only as a scarf only. Eight people are not wearing gloves and seven are not wearing a scarf. One more person can be seen wearing all three than wearing a hat only.

181. How many people are wearing hat, scarf and gloves?
182. How many people are wearing gloves only?
183. How many people are wearing a scarf only?
184. How many people are wearing a hat and gloves but no scarf?
185. How many people are wearing gloves?
186. How many people can be seen in the picture?

OBSTACLE 24 In break-time at a shop children can buy chips, candy and soda. Two more children buy candy only than chips only. Thirty-seven children do not buy any candy at all. Two more children buy both chips and soda but no candy than candy only. A total of 60 children buy soda, but only nine of them have soda only. Twelve children buy chips only. One more child buys candy only than candy and soda only, and three more buy both chips and candy but no soda than buy chips and soda but no candy.

187. How many children buy all three items?
188. How many children buy chips and candy but no soda?
189. How many children buy chips and soda but no candy?
190. How many children visit the shop?
191. How many children do not have chips?
192. How many children have candy only?

Answers on page 27

ZONE 1

OBSTACLE 25 Sausage, fries and beans are being served to 22 people. The same number have sausage and fries only as sausage and beans only. Only seven do not have fries. The same number have fries and beans only as fries only. Twice as many have beans and sausage but no fries as have sausage only. One person has beans only and one more person has sausage, fries and beans than sausage and fries only.

193. How many people have sausage, fries and beans?
194. How many people have sausage only?
195. How many people do not have beans?
196. How many people do not have sausage?
197. How many people have fries and beans but no sausage?
198. How many people have sausage and fries only?

OBSTACLE 26 On sports day the fastest runners are taking part in the sprint, the hurdles and the relay. One more person takes part in the hurdles only than the sprint only. The same number take part in the sprint and the hurdles as take part in the relay and the hurdles. Eleven of the athletes taking some part in these three races do not do the relay. Five people take part in the sprint and the relay and three enter all three races. There are four teams of four runners in the relay. One more person is running in both the relay and the sprint than in the hurdles only.

199. How many people are taking some part in any of the three races?
200. How many people are taking part in the relay only?
201. How many people do not take part in the hurdles?
202. How many people do not take part in the sprint?
203. How many people take part in both the hurdles and relay but not the sprint?
204. How many people take part in two races only?

(Answers on pages 27 & 28)

ZONE 1

OBSTACLE 27 A survey has been carried out on TV viewing. The survey shows the percentages of people who watch soaps, documentaries and movies. 26% of people watch all three. 39% of people do not watch documentaries. The percentage of people watching soaps only plus the percentage of people watching movies only is the same as the number who watch both movies and documentaries. 27% of people do not watch movies, 14% watch both soaps and documentaries and 3% watch documentaries only.

205. What percentage of people watch both soaps and movies but no documentaries?
206. What percentage watch soaps only?
207. What percentage watch movies and documentaries but not soaps?
208. What percentage watch movies only?
209. What percentage watch only two out of the three types of show?
210. What percentage watch only one type of show?

OBSTACLE 28 At a pick-your-own fruit farm, twice as many people are picking raspberries only as plums only. Three more people pick strawberries, raspberries and plums as pick plums only. Four more people pick strawberries only as pick both raspberries and strawberries but not plums. 50 people do not pick strawberries. Eleven people pick both plums and raspberries but not strawberries. A total of 60 people pick plums. If the total number of fruit pickers is 100, can you answer the questions below?

211. How many people pick raspberries?
212. How many people pick all three?
213. How many people pick raspberries only?
214. How many people pick both plums and strawberries but no raspberries?
215. How many people pick strawberries only?
216. How many people pick only two of the three fruits?

Answers on page 28

ZONE 1

THE DEDUCTION CRAWL

OBSTACLE 29 At a college teaching crafts, sciences and humanities, the new intake of students can study a maximum of two of the three subjects. One more student is studying a craft and a humanities than a craft only. Two more are studying both a science and a humanities than are studying both a craft and a science. Half as many are studying both a craft and a humanities as are studying both a craft and a science. 21 students are not doing a craft subject. Three students are studying a humanities subject only and six are studying a science only.

217. How many students are not studying a science?
218. How many students are studying both a science and humanities?
219. How many students are studying two subjects?
220. How many students are studying only one subject?
221. How many students are not doing a humanities subject?
222. How many students are studying a craft only?

OBSTACLE 30 At a kennel there are Labradors, Alsatians and Greyhounds and also crosses of these breeds. There are two more true Labradors than true Alsatians. Six dogs are Alsatian and Labrador crosses. Ten dogs have no Labrador or Alsatian in them. Only one dog is a mixture of all three breeds. There are twice as many Labrador and Alsatian crosses than Labrador and Greyhound crosses. There is one more Alsatian and Greyhound cross than Labrador and Greyhound cross. Twenty-two dogs do not have any Alsatian in them. There are 40 dogs in total in the kennels.

223. How many true Labradors are there?
224. How many true Alsatians are there?
225. How many true Greyhounds are there?
226. How many Labrador and Greyhound crosses are there?
227. How many Alsatian and Greyhound crosses are there?
228. How many dogs do not have any Labrador in them?

OBSTACLE 31 What word has a similar meaning to the first word and rhymes with the second word?

229.	FRUIT	—	GATE	230.	PRICE	—	LOST
231.	STOPPER	—	FORK	232.	LEAN	—	SHIN
233.	SPHERE	—	WALL	234.	LINK	—	FOND
235.	INSTRUMENT	—	CARP	236.	FACE	—	TILE
237.	GROOVE	—	BLOT	238.	LOAN	—	SEND

Answers on page 29

The Mensa Mind Obstacle Course

SCORING SYSTEM

Compare your scores in each section against the scoring charts. If you are under 16 years old you must add the bonus points for your age grouping.

The aim is to find out how intelligent you are and the most intelligent are given promotions on the completion of each Zone. Score 1 point for each correct answer.

The list of ratings or ranks for the Mind Obstacle Course are given below. You can get promoted or demoted as you advance through the zones. Only the very highest intellects will make it to Five Star Generals.

Structure of Ranks in the Mensa Mind Army

Private "Third Class"
Private "Second Class"
Private "First Class"
Acting Corporal
Corporal
Sergeant   –   **Average Intelligence Level**
Master Sergeant
Second Lieutenant
Lieutenant
Captain
Major   –   **High Intelligence Level**
Lieutenant Colonel
Colonel
General   (One Star)   –   **Very High Intelligence Level**
               (Two Star)
               (Three Star)
               (Four Star)
               (Five Star)

If you have scored Major or higher it is recommended that you contact your National Mensa for their IQ assessment test (see page 4 for details).

ZONE 1

ANSWERS

OBSTACLE 1

1. A.	2. D.	3. L.	4. O.	5. N.
6. H.	7. K.	8. R.	9. T.	10. S.
11. V.	12. C.	13. U.	14. I.	15. B.
16. M.	17. G.	18. F.	19. E.	20. P.

OBSTACLE 2

21. S, to make Allow, Basil.
22. C, to make Pith, Scale.
23. P, to make Ride, Slope.
24. M, to make Swap, Clamp.
25. T, to make Sill, Facet.
26. H, to make Tree, Niche.
    Or R, to make Thee, Nicer.
27. U, to make Vale, Cause.
28. E, to make What, Feast.
29. N, to make Moth, Gland.
30. T, to make Meal, Hotly.
31. R, to make Wing, First.
32. T, to make Wine, Comet.
33. U, to make Prod, Bound.
34. R, to make Dated, Breach.
35. V, to make Cured, Shove
36. R, to make Cease, Brand.
37. N, to make Bugle, Canter.
38. G, to make Bride, Finger.
39. A, to make Twin, Haunt.
40. O, to make Stop, Float.

OBSTACLE 3

41. Break.
42. Base.
43. Rest.
44. Tuba.
45. Real.
46. Back.
47. Ring.
48. Rust.
49. Sand.
50. Strand.

ZONE 1

THE DEDUCTION CRAWL

OBSTACLE 4

51. 14.
52. 7.
53. 2 (using segment numbers 1, 6, 7, 9, 11, 12 and 1, 4, 6, 10, 12).
54. 18.

OBSTACLE 5

The aisle order is: 1. fruit, 2. tins, 3. washing powder, 4. bottles, 5. meat, 6. bread.

55. Bread.
56. Four.
57. Fruit.
58. Two.

OBSTACLE 6

From one end or the other, the order is: white, green, black, red, silver, yellow, blue, purple.

59. Silver.
60. Red.
61. Blue.
62. Yellow.

OBSTACLE 7

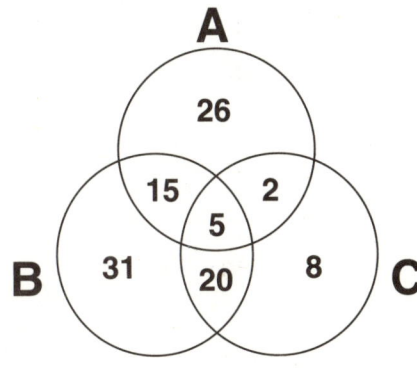

A = Hotel, B = Self-Catering, C = Camping.

63. 26.   **64.** 15.   **65.** 36.   **66.** 37.

Answers

ZONE 1

OBSTACLE 8

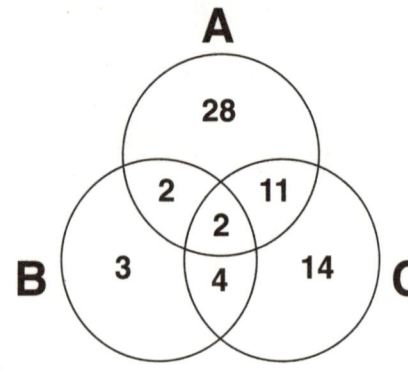

A = Thriller, B = Biography, C = Science Fiction.

67. 11.   **68.** 17.   **69.** 2.   **70.** 28.

OBSTACLE 9

71.	Curl.	72.	Barrier.
73.	Camembert.	74.	Calorie.
75.	Dawn.	76.	Dupe.
77.	Epidemic.	78.	Epistle.
79.	Fairyland.	80.	Falter.
81.	Golf.	82.	Grain.
83.	Herringbone.	84.	Hessian.
85.	Immediate.	86.	Joint.
87.	Kipper.	88.	League.
89.	Limerick.	90.	Mediate.

OBSTACLE 10

91. D.   **92.** E.   **93.** A.   **94.** C.   **95.** B.

OBSTACLE 11

96. B.   **97.** D.   **98.** E.   **99.** C.   **100.** A.

ZONE 1

THE DEDUCTION CRAWL

OBSTACLE 12

101. E.   **102.** A.   **103.** D.   **104.** B.   **105.** C.

OBSTACLE 13

106. D.   **107.** C.   **108.** B.   **109.** E.   **110.** A.

OBSTACLE 14

111. F.   **112.** B.   **113.** E.   **114.** F.   **115.** C.

OBSTACLE 15

116. Four.   **117.** 26th.
118. 15th.   **119.** Thursday.
120. Tuesday.

OBSTACLE 16

Kerry has a striped jumper, plain shirt and spotted towel; Paul has a spotted jumper, striped shirt and plain towel; Sandra has a plain jumper, spotted shirt and striped towel.

121. Paul.   **122.** Striped.
123. Paul.   **124.** Striped.
125. Plain.

OBSTACLE 17

Joanna has a cat on her pen, a rabbit on her crayon and an elephant on her pencil-case; Richard has a rabbit on his pen, an elephant on his crayon and a cat on his pencil-case; Thomas has an elephant on his pen, a cat on his crayon and a rabbit on his pencil-case.

126. Joanna.   **127.** Elephant.
128. Thomas.   **129.** Rabbit.
130. Joanna.

Answers

25

ZONE 1

THE DEDUCTION CRAWL

OBSTACLE 18

131. 28. (x 3) + 1.
132. 6. (– 5) x 2.
133. 11. (x 2) + 7.
134. 22. (x 2) – 2.
135. 13. (÷ 2) + 6.
136. 17. (– 7) ÷ 2.
137. 20. (– 4) x 2.
138. 20. (squared) + 4.
139. 8. (√) + 3.
140. 4. (squared) – 5.
141. 80. (+ 8) x 5.
142. 36. (– 11) x 4.
143. 62. (x 6) + 8.
144. 71. (x 4) – 13.
145. 13. (÷ 4) + 3.
146. 19. (÷ 5) – 3.
147. 36. (– 13) x 6.
148. 162. (+ 3) x 9.
149. 361. + 2, then squared.
150. 6. – 4, then √.

OBSTACLE 19

151. 6.   **152.** 6.   **153.** 5.   **154.** 14.   **155.** 4.

OBSTACLE 20

156. A.   **157.** C.   **158.** B.   **159.** C.   **160.** C.

OBSTACLE 21

161. Appear.
162. Above.
163. Acquire.
164. Acquit.
165. Acerbity.
166. Absent.
167. Actual.
168. Abbreviate.
169. Airy.
170. Adult.

OBSTACLE 22

171. Humdrum.
172. Humorous.
173. Humiliate.
174. Hostile.
175. Headstrong.
176. Hold.
177. Hopeful.
178. Hardship.
179. Hero.
180. Hungry.

Answers

ZONE 1

OBSTACLE 23

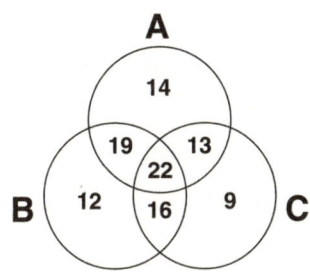

A = Hat, B = Scarf, C = Gloves.

181. 3. **182.** 1. **183.** 1.
184. 4. **185.** 10. **186.** 18.

OBSTACLE 24

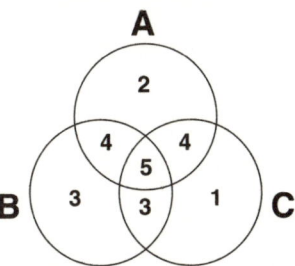

A = Candy, B = Chips, C = Soda.

187. 22. **188.** 19. **189.** 16.
190. 105. **191.** 36. **192.** 14.

OBSTACLE 25

A = Sausage, B = Fries, C = Beans.

193. 5. **194.** 2. **195.** 9.
196. 7. **197.** 3. **198.** 4.

Answers

ZONE 1

THE DEDUCTION CRAWL

OBSTACLE 26

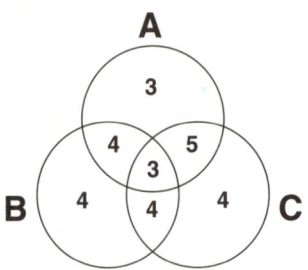

A = Sprint, B = Hurdles, C = Relay.

199. 27. **200.** 4. **201.** 12.
202. 12. **203.** 4. **204.** 13.

OBSTACLE 27

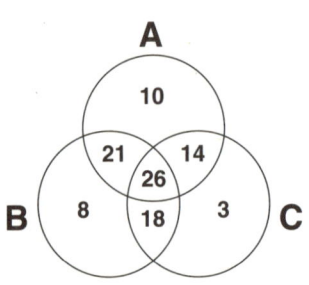

A = Soaps, B = Movies, C = Documentaries.

205. 21. **206.** 10. **207.** 18.
208. 8. **209.** 53. **210.** 21.

OBSTACLE 28

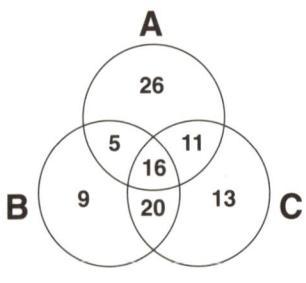

A = Raspberries, B = Strawberries, C = Plums.

211. 58. **212.** 16. **213.** 26.
214. 20. **215.** 9. **216.** 36.

Answers

ZONE 1

OBSTACLE 29

A = Craft, B = Science, C = Humanities.

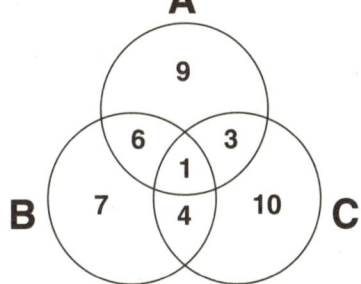

| 217. | 12. | 218. | 12. | 219. | 27. |
| 220. | 13. | 221. | 20. | 222. | 4. |

OBSTACLE 30

A = Labrador, B = Alsatian, C = Greyhound.

| 223. | 9. | 224. | 7. | 225. | 10. |
| 226. | 3. | 227. | 4. | 228. | 21. |

OBSTACLE 31

229. Date.
230. Cost.
231. Cork.
232. Thin.
233. Ball.
234. Bond.
235. Harp.
236. Dial.
237. Slot.
238. Lend.

29

SCORING SYSTEM

How did you fare?

Promotion Criteria (See page 21):

Under 120	*"Back to Boot Camp"*. Private "Third Class".
121 - 150	*"Pass Boot Camp"*. Private "Second Class".
151 - 190	Private "First Class".
191 - 220	Acting Corporal.
221+	Corporal.

If you are under 16 don't forget to add your Age Bonus Points

Age in Years	10	10.5	11	11.5	12	12.5	13	13.5	14	14.5	15	15.5
Bonus Points	40	35	30	25	20	18	16	18	12	10	8	4

ZONE ②

A spring in the step and a clear head will be required to leap over this set of 152 mathematical hurdles.

THE NUMBER JUMP

OBSTACLE 1   Six children have invented a card game and scoring system. It uses the cards up to 10, at face value, with aces scoring 1. In each round, the value of the card dealt is added to that child's score. Diamonds are worth double the face value. If two or more children are dealt cards with the same face value in one round, they lose the value of the that card instead of gaining it(diamonds still doubled). They are each dealt six cards face up as shown below:

Player	Round 1	Round 2	Round 3	Round 4	Round 5	Round 6
1	6 ♥	3 ♠	ACE ♦	9 ♣	10 ♥	4 ♠
2	10 ♠	ACE ♠	7 ♥	6 ♦	5 ♠	8 ♣
3	7 ♦	8 ♥	4 ♣	3 ♥	ACE ♣	5 ♣
4	4 ♥	9 ♦	7 ♠	5 ♦	10 ♣	3 ♦
5	8 ♠	5 ♥	6 ♠	9 ♠	2 ♠	4 ♦
6	3 ♣	2 ♣	9 ♥	7 ♣	10 ♦	8 ♦

When the scores are added up, which player:

1. Came third?
2. Won?
3. Came last?
4. Was winning after the fourth cards had been dealt?
5. Had even scores?
6. Had a score divisible by 3?
7. What was the second highest score?
8. What was the sum of all of the scores?

Answers on page 60

ZONE 2

OBSTACLE 2 A farmer keeps only four types of animals. He has a total of 560 animals. If he had 10 sheep less he would have twice as many sheep as he has cows. If he had 10 cows less he would have three cows for every pig, and he has two and one half pigs to every horse.

9. How many pigs does he have?
10. How many horses does he have?
11. If he swaps 75% of his cows for 7 sheep per cow, how many animals will he have in total?
12. How many sheep will he have after the swap?

OBSTACLE 3

13. What number should replace the symbols in this grid if only the numbers 1 to 7 can be used?

□	□	△	○	★	14
★	○	△	○	◉	19
□	○	◉	◐	○	23
○	★	◉	★	★	9
◐	◐	★	■	○	23
16	15	19	18	20	?

OBSTACLE 4 What numbers should replace the question marks in the series below?

14. 7   9   16   25   41   ?
15. 4   14   34   74   ?
16. 2   3   5   5   9   7   14   ?   ?
17. 6   9   15   27   ?
18. 11   7   –1   –17   ?
19. 8   15   26   43   ?
20. 3.5   4   7   14   49   ?

32   Answers on Pages 60 & 61

ZONE 2

THE NUMBER JUMP

OBSTACLE 5 What numbers are missing from these number grids?

21.

A	B	C	D	E
7	5	3	4	8
9	8	8	8	8
6	4	9	3	5
8	3	6	?	9

22.

A	B	C	D	E
7	8	7	9	7
5	5	8	5	9
6	3	7	3	9
4	4	8	6	?

23.

A	B	C	D	E
3	5	4	6	3
4	8	5	9	7
6	1	5	4	6
2	2	?	1	4

Answers on page 61

ZONE 2

OBSTACLE 6 — What numbers should replace the question marks?

24.

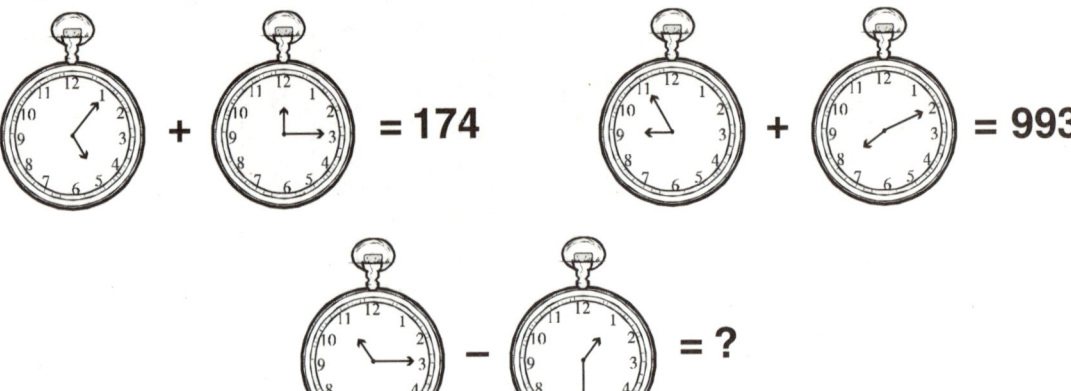

25.

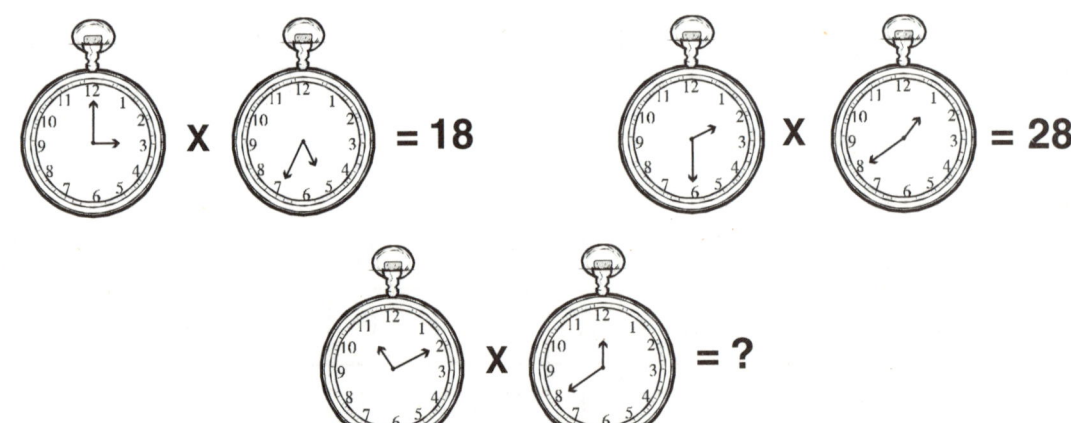

Answers on page 61

ZONE 2

THE NUMBER JUMP

26.

27.

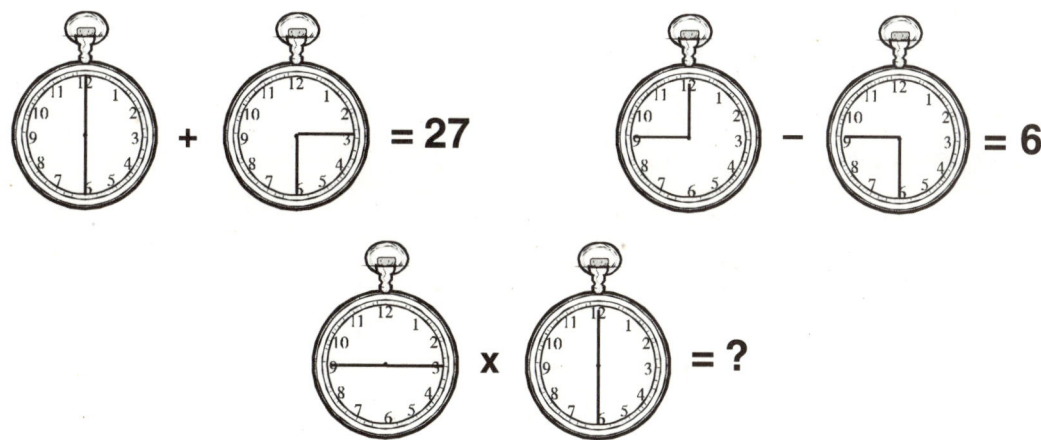

Answers on page 61

35

ZONE 2

THE NUMBER JUMP

OBSTACLE 7 The numbers in box 1 move clockwise to the positions shown in box 2. In which positions should the missing numbers appear?

28.

1

2	6	7
11		1
10	3	5

2

	10	
7		2
	11	

29.

1

22	15	34
12		14
23	21	19

2

14		12
19		23

30.

1

3	5	8
1		6
17	7	9

2

	1	
5		8
	7	

Answers on pages 61 & 62

36

ZONE 2

OBSTACLE 8 What numbers should replace the question marks?

31.

7534	41	3
9624	72	5
5816	42	?

32.

3569	2307	104
7678	5426	380
9925	4185	?

33.

6225	1210	20
7946	6324	188
3483	1224	?

Answers on page 62

THE NUMBER JUMP

37

ZONE 2

OBSTACLE 9 Divide these two grids into four identical shapes. The sum of the numbers contained within each of the shapes must give the totals shown.

34. Totals **120**

8	7	6	8	7	12	9	1
7	12	7	6	4	3	2	14
8	9	7	8	5	7	11	1
8	8	10	7	6	16	10	1
4	9	13	4	12	2	15	6
8	5	2	2	4	9	8	15
6	9	8	14	14	8	2	1
9	6	10	5	12	1	5	17

35. Totals **134**

5	7	8	15	4	7	5	6
11	6	9	8	16	12	10	10
7	12	10	12	3	11	6	8
6	7	2	5	7	7	15	10
12	15	10	8	5	12	8	7
6	7	11	13	9	6	9	6
9	8	10	6	8	8	1	2
3	6	4	10	10	10	15	15

THE NUMBER JUMP

Answers on page 62

ZONE 2

OBSTACLE 10 The values of grids A and B are given. What is the value of the grid C?

36.

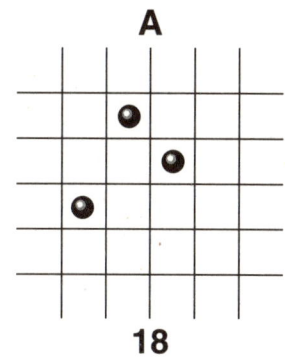 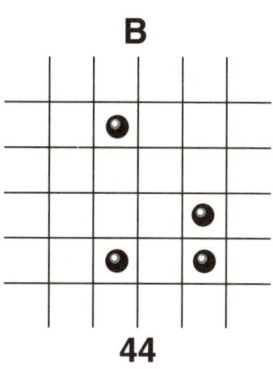 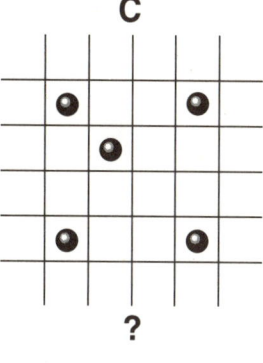

37.

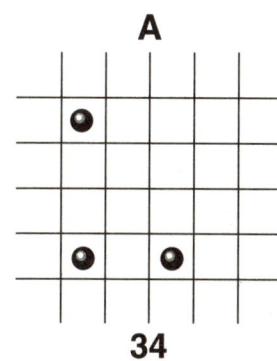 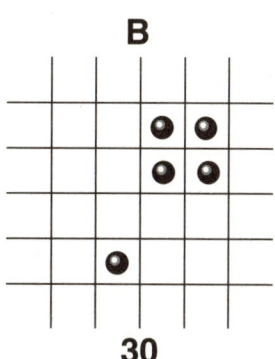 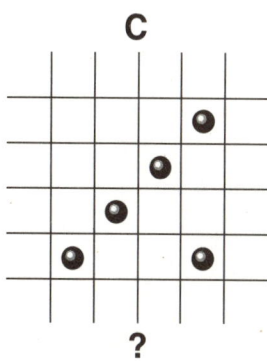

A triangle denotes the grid value and a circle denotes twice the grid value. The values of grids A and B are given. What is the value of the grid C?

38.

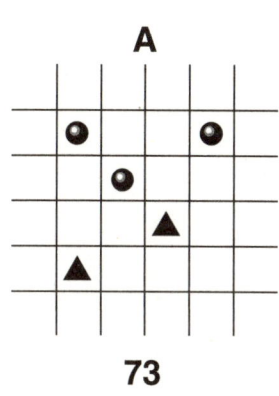 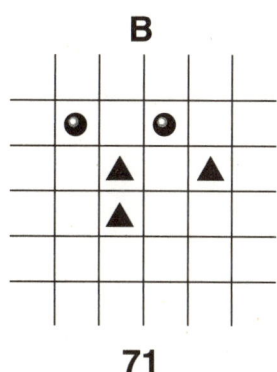 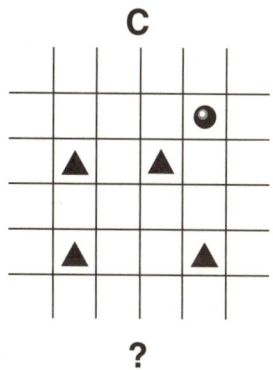

Answers on page 63

ZONE 2

THE NUMBER JUMP

OBSTACLE 11 Can you calculate the numbers missing in the figures below? Each number is used once only and is not reversed.

39.

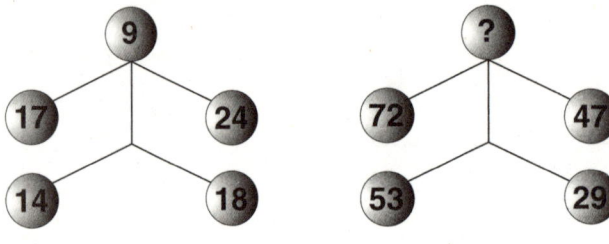

40.

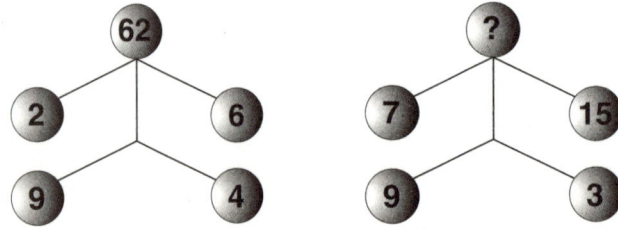

41.

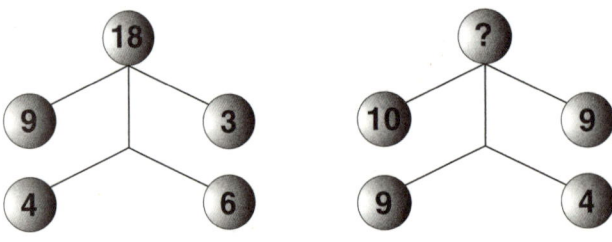

42.

Answers on page 63

ZONE 2

THE NUMBER JUMP

43.

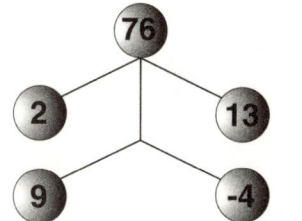 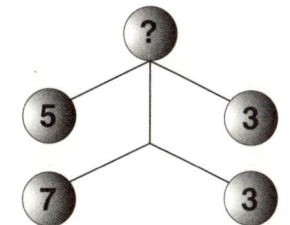

44.

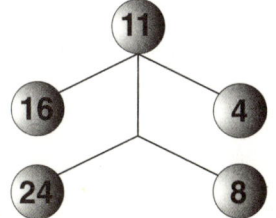 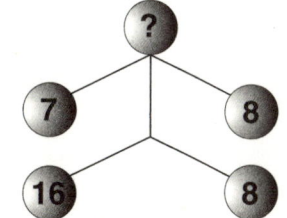

45.

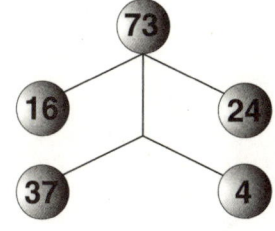 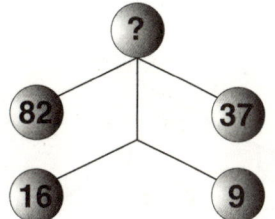

46.

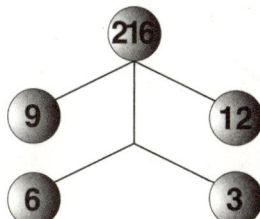 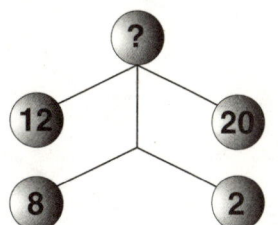

Answers on page 63

ZONE 2

THE NUMBER JUMP

47.

48.

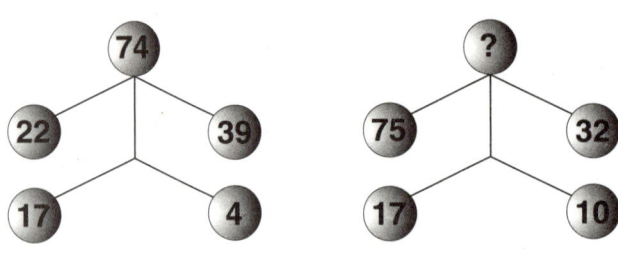

OBSTACLE 12 Starting at the top number, find a route that goes down one level each time until you reach the bottom number.

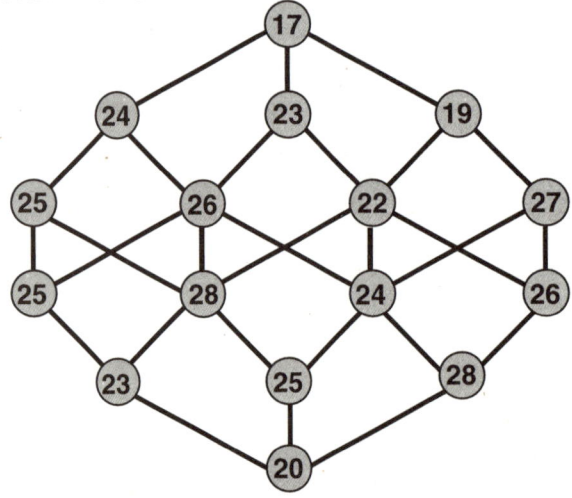

49. Can you find a route where the sum of the numbers is 130?
50. Can you find two separate routes that give a total of 131?
51. What is the highest possible score and what route/s do you follow?
52. What is the lowest possible score and what route/s do you follow?
53. How many ways are there to score 136 and what route/s do you follow?

Answers on page 63

ZONE 2

THE NUMBER JUMP

OBSTACLE 13   Starting at the top number, find a route that goes down one level each time until you reach the bottom number.

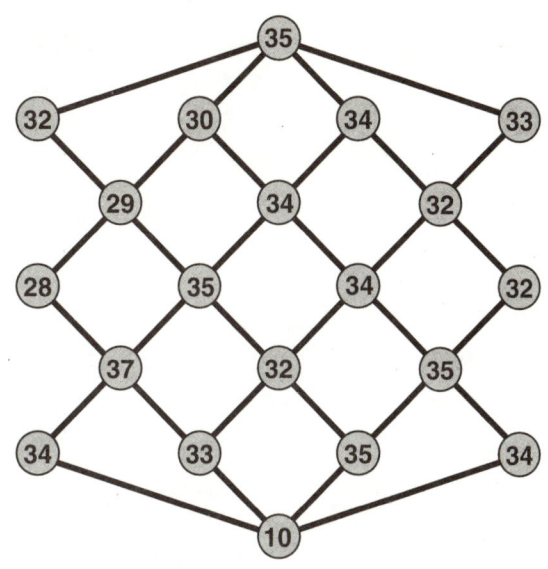

54.   Can you find a route where the sum of the numbers is 216?
55.   Can you find two separate routes that give a total of 204?
56.   What is the highest possible score and what route/s do you follow?
57.   What is the lowest possible score and what route/s do you follow?
58.   How many ways are there to score 211 and what route/s do you follow?

OBSTACLE 14   What is the value of the last string in each of these problems if the first three strings have values as given? Black, white and shaded circles have different values.

59.

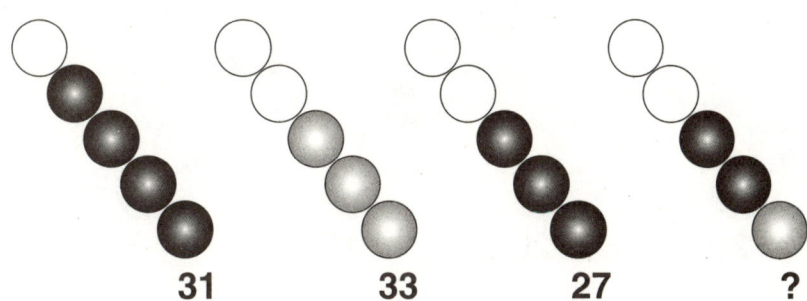

Answers on page 64

43

ZONE 2

THE NUMBER JUMP

60.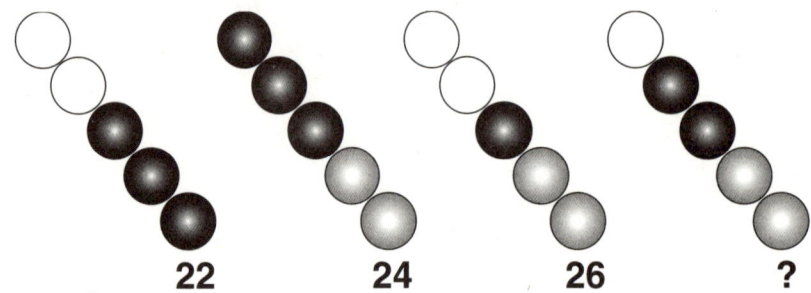
22   24   26   ?

61.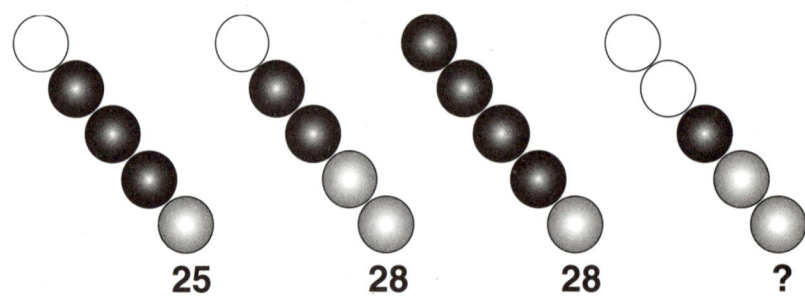
25   28   28   ?

62.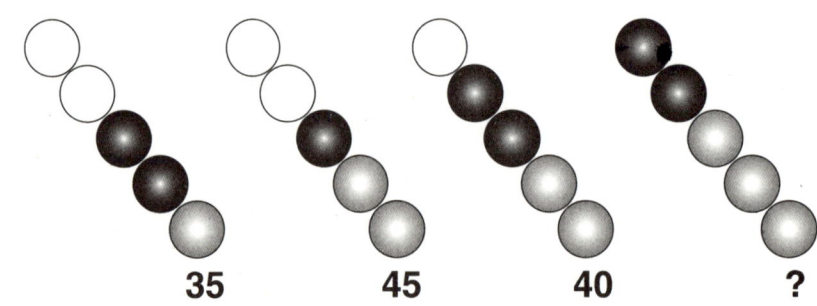
35   45   40   ?

63.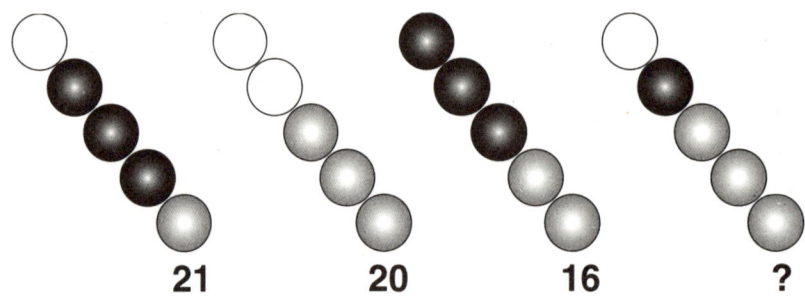
21   20   16   ?

Answers on page 64

44

ZONE 2

THE NUMBER JUMP

64. 21 21 20 ?

65. 22 13 19 ?

66. 29 22 17 ?

67. 30 18 40 ?

Answers on page 64

ZONE 2

THE NUMBER JUMP

68.

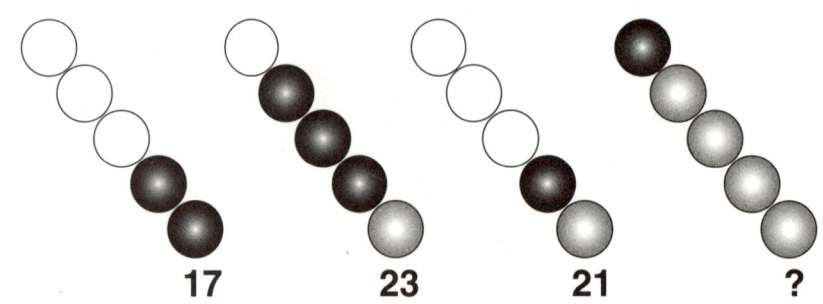

17   23   21   ?

OBSTACLE 15 The numbers on the grids below are found by giving the value of any symbol that is adjacent horizontally, vertically or diagonally. The numbers are then halved in adjacent boxes. If there is more than one value that can go in a box, then they are added together. See examples below.

	A	B	C	D	E	F
1	2	2	2	2	0	0
2	4	4	4	2	0	0
3	4	×	4	2	0	0
4	4	4	4	2	0	0
5	2	2	2	2	0	0
6	0	0	0	0	0	0

\+

	A	B	C	D	E	F
1	0	5	5	5	5	5
2	0	5	10	10	10	5
3	0	5	10	△	10	5
4	0	5	10	10	10	5
5	0	5	5	5	5	5
6	0	0	0	0	0	0

=

	A	B	C	D	E	F
1	2	7	7	7	5	5
2	4	9	14	12	10	5
3	4	×	14	△	10	5
4	4	9	14	12	10	5
5	2	7	7	7	5	5
6	0	0	0	0	0	0

If × = 4 & △ = 10

The grid value would look like the example

$$C1 = (D3 \times \tfrac{1}{2}) + (B3 \times \tfrac{1}{2}) = 7$$
$$A5 = B3 \times \tfrac{1}{2} = 2$$
$$D4 = D3 + (B3 \times \tfrac{1}{2}) = 12$$

Answers on page 64

ZONE 2

THE NUMBER JUMP

From the information in the grid below, complete the grid and answer the questions that follow:

	A	B	C	D	E	F
1						
2	32	●			T	16
3			□			
4		T			□	
5					●	
6			22			28

69. What is the value of square D1?
70. What is the value of square A3?
71. What is the value of square F3?
72. What square has the highest value?
73. What is the value of □?
74. What is the value of the lowest square?
75. What are the values of the symbols ● and T?
76. Which 3 squares have a value of 32?

Now try this more difficult grid using the same rules:

	A	B	C	D	E	F
1	△					24
2			★	△	△	
3	37		⊗			
4					⊗	
5		⊗				
6				△		20

77. What are the values of the three symbols?
78. What is the value of the highest square?
79. What is the value of square C4?
80. What is the value of the lowest square?
81. What is the value of square E3?
82. How many squares have a value of 64?

Answers on page 64

47

ZONE 2

OBSTACLE 16 Start at the top-left circle and move clockwise. Calculate the number that replaces the question marks in the following:

83.
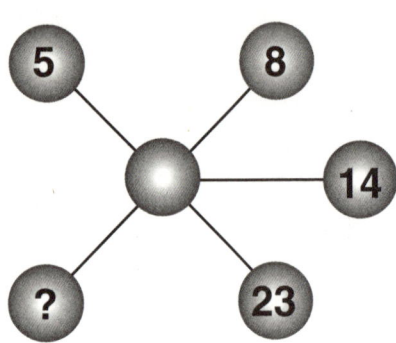

84.
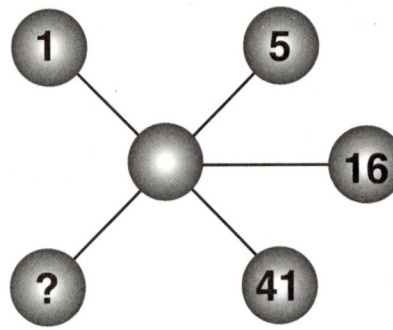

85.
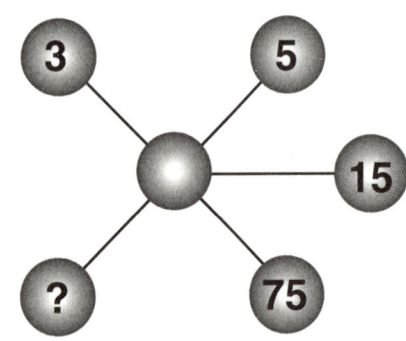

86.
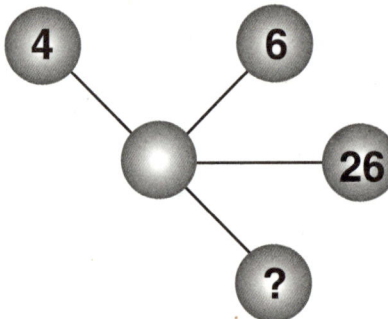

87.
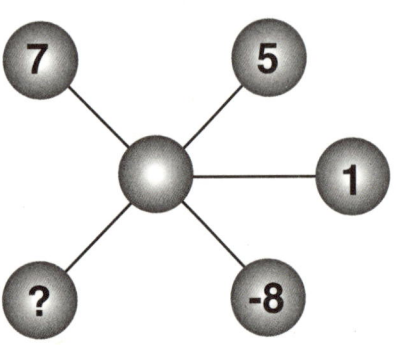

88.
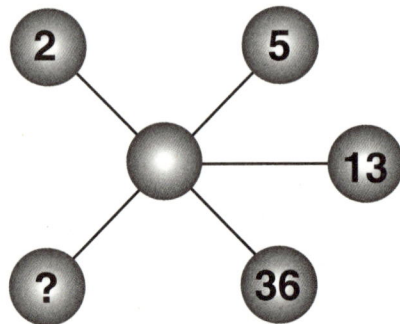

Answers on page 65

ZONE 2

THE NUMBER JUMP

89.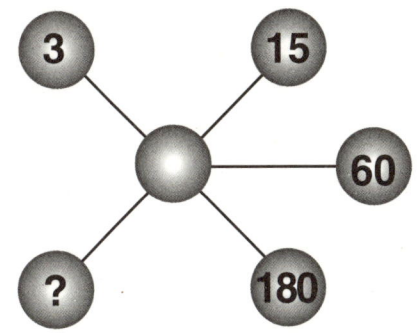

90.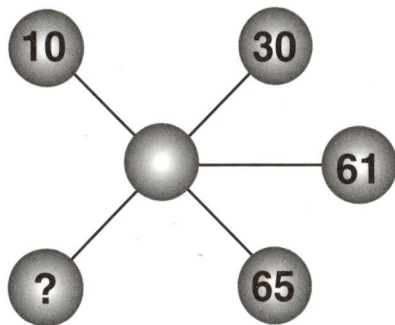

91.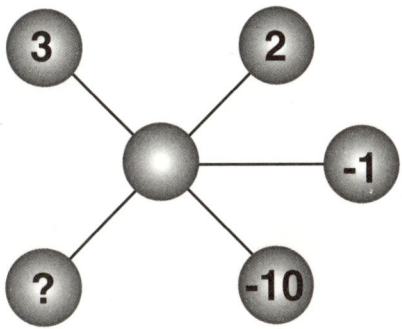

92.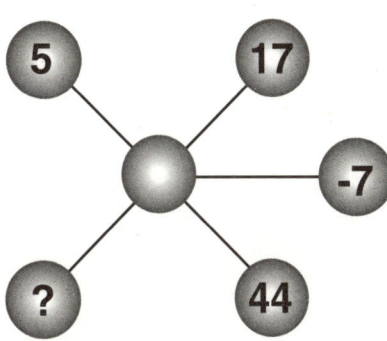

93.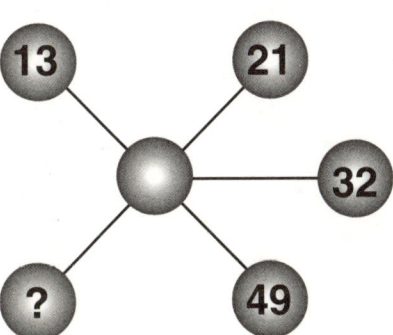

94.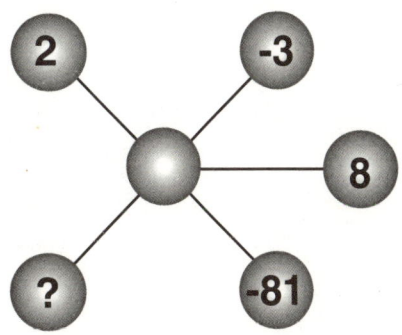

Answers on page 65

ZONE 2

THE NUMBER JUMP

95.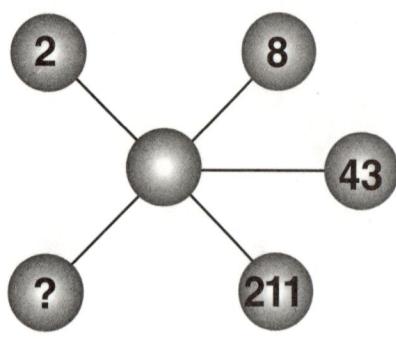

96.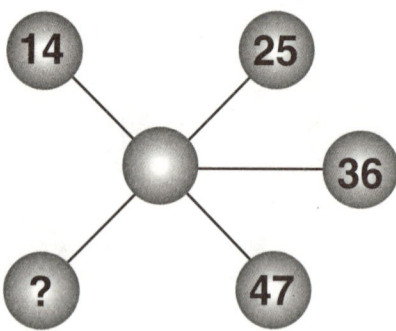

97.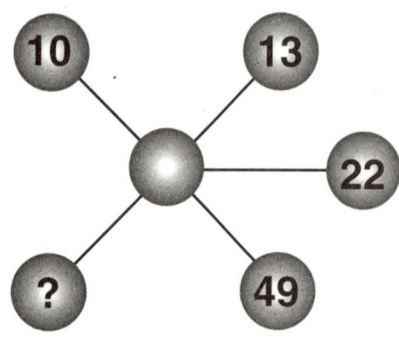

98.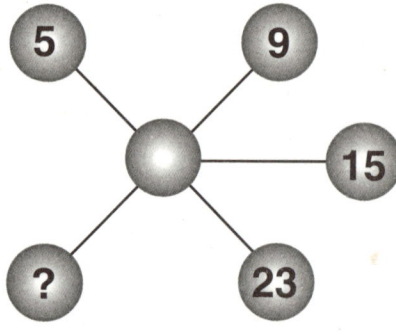

99.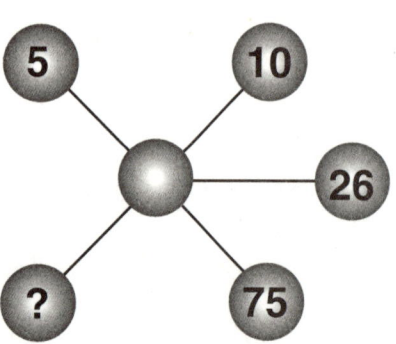

100.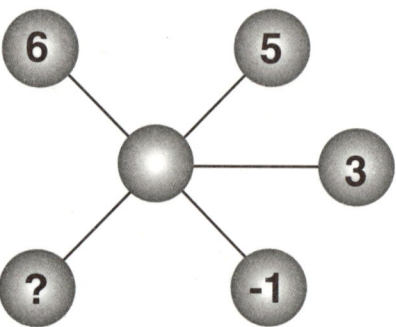

Answers on page 65

ZONE 2

THE NUMBER JUMP

101.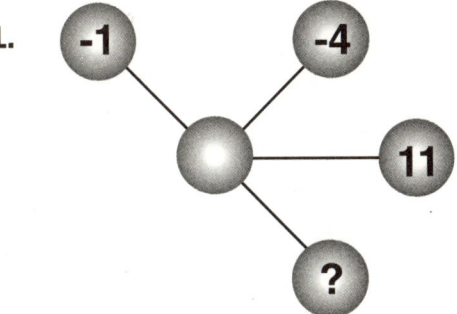

102.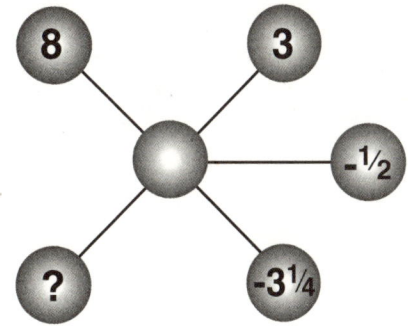

OBSTACLE 17 The number in the middle knot of the following bow ties is reached by using all of the outer numbers only once. You cannot reverse the numbers to obtain the answers. Which numbers should replace the question marks?

103.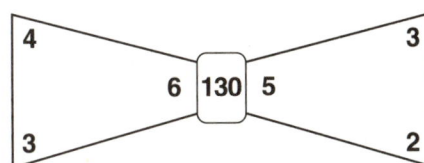

104.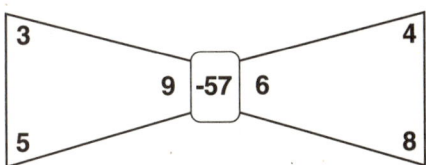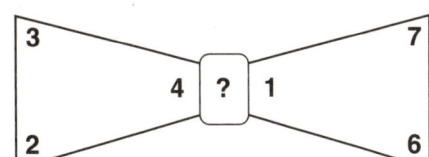

105.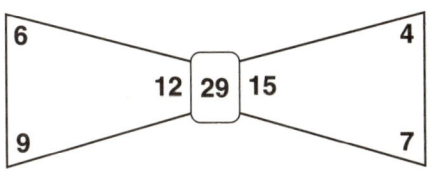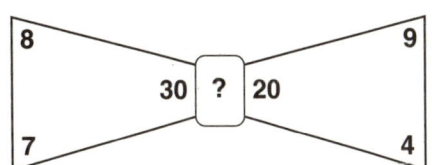

Answers on page 65

51

ZONE 2

THE NUMBER JUMP

106.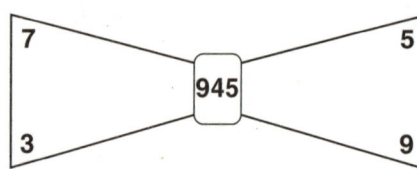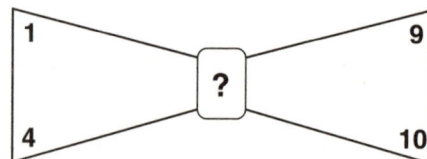

107.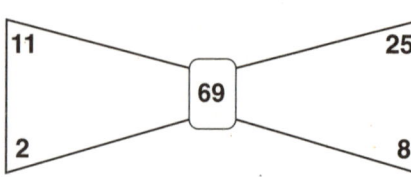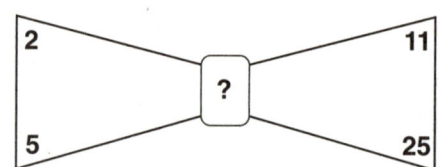

108.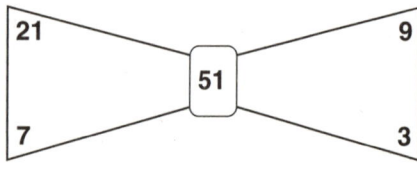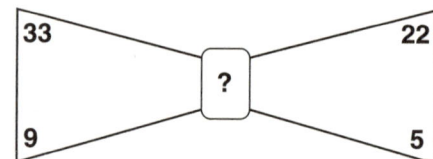

Answers on page 65

ZONE 2

THE NUMBER JUMP

OBSTACLE 18 In the grid below, the intersections have a value equal to the sum of their four touching numbers.

```
    A  B  C  D  E  F  G
   30 19 28 26 25 36 16 29
 1
   24 20 26 23 24 23 24 22
 2
   26 29 27 20 25 29 27 23
 3
   20 23 28 32 29 30 24 22
 4
   30 28 27 22 30 26 27 29
 5
   20 28 23 28 32 29 31 26
 6
   25 27 25 27 30 26 24 19
 7
   26 26 29 23 24 28 24 28
```

Can you answer the following:

109. What are the grid references for the three intersection points with a value of 100?

110. Which intersection point/s has a value of 92?

111. How many intersections have a value of less than 100?

112. Which intersection has the highest value?

113. Which intersection has the lowest value?

114. Which intersection/s has a value of 115?

115. How many intersections have a value of 105 and which are they?

116. How many intersections have a value of 111 and which are they?

OBSTACLE 19 Can you find the missing values on the roofs of the following houses? Each of the numbers on the windows and door must be used only once and no number can be reversed.

117.

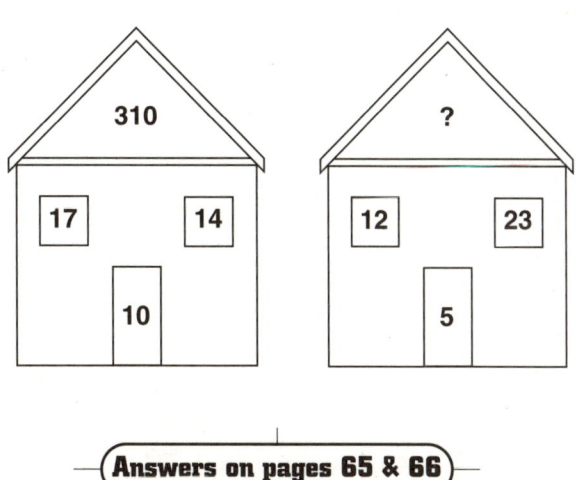

(Answers on pages 65 & 66)

53

ZONE 2

THE NUMBER JUMP

118.

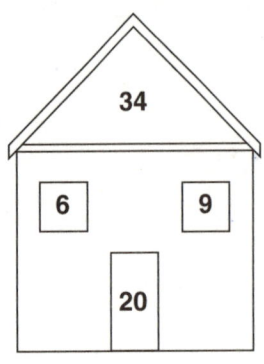 

119.

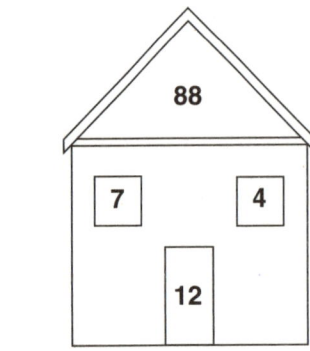 

120.

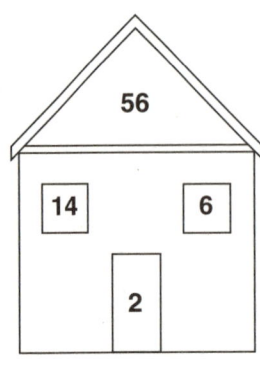 

Answers on page 66

121.

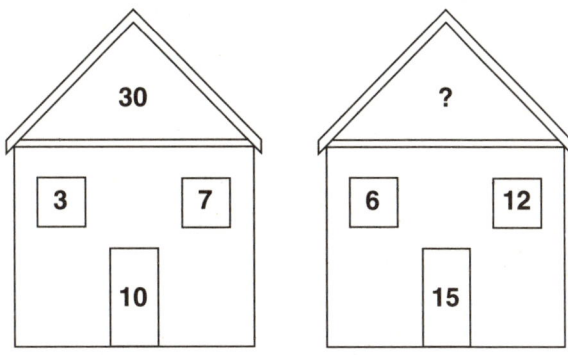

122.

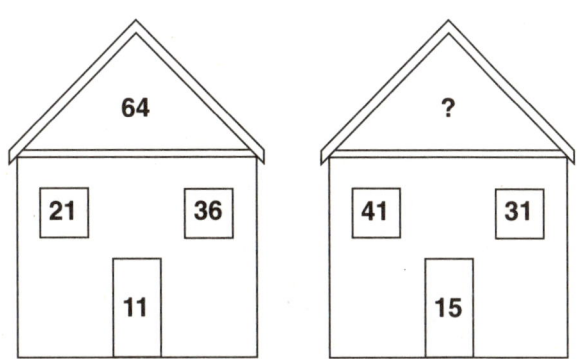

OBSTACLE 20

123. If two-thirds of a number is three-quarters of $42^{2/3}$, what is that number?

124. If half the square root of a number is one-fifth of 20, what is that number?

125. If half of a positive number is squared and is then halved again, and it is equal to the original number, what is that number?

126. If a quarter of a number is equal to the cube root of 512, what is that number?

127. If 50% of a positive number is equal to twice the square root of that number, what is that number?

Answers on page 66

55

ZONE 2

128. If twice a number is squared and it is equal to one-half of 50, what is that number?

129. If 3 is subtracted from a number and the remainder is squared, it is 45 less than the original number squared. What was that number?

130. If 10 times a number is the square root of another number that is 1000 times the number, what is that number?

131. If 26 times a number is 1/26 of 4 x 50, what is that number?

132. If 40 times a number is half of 7 x 8 x 10, what is that number?

133. How can 0.18 + 0.19 relate to a lion?

134. What two whole numbers squared add up to 50?

135. A shopkeeper has a full box of nails that contains 8200 nails. He also has 250 packets of 12 nails, 200 packets of 24 nails, 180 packets of 10 nails and 372 assorted loose nails. How many more nails can he put in the box?

136. Simon had a bag of candy. When he tried to divide them into three piles he had one left over. The same happened when he tried to divide them into four, five and six piles. But when he split them into seven piles he had none left over. How many candies did he start with?

137. A number contains eight digits, two each of 1, 2, 3 and 4. The 1s are separated by one digit, the 2s by two digits, the 3s by three digits and the 4s by four digits. Reconstruct the number to give an answer that can be read in either direction.

138. A man playing roulette had a winning streak. Each time he won he gambled half of his total money at odds that would double his stake if he won. He started with $64 and after eight spins he had $546.75. What was his sequence of wins and losses?

139. What is the value of x, if x is a whole number, in the sum below?

$$x^3 + (2x)^2 = 8 \times 3$$

ZONE 2

OBSTACLE 21 What numbers are missing from the segments below?

140.

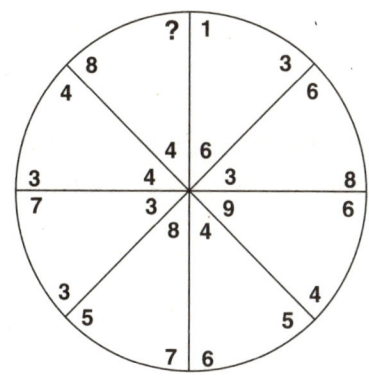

141.

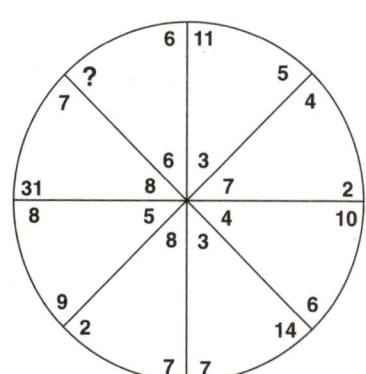

142.

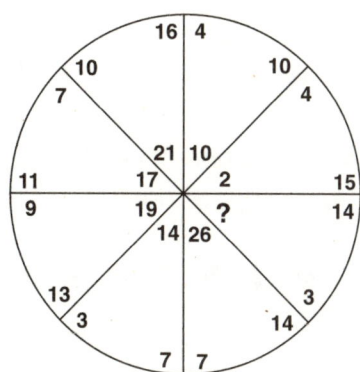

Answers on page 66

ZONE 2

OBSTACLE 22

143. If Alan gives Brenda $5.50 they will both have the same amount of money. If Brenda gives Alan $1.50, Alan will have twice as much as Brenda. What did they have at the start?

144. A child has an equal number of four different coins from 1c, 5c, 10c, 25c, 50c, and $1. If the total value is $20.28, then how many of which coins does the child have?

145. Divide 100 by one-half, and add 7. What is the answer?

146. A cube 8in x 8in x 8in is immersed in paint and then cut into half-inch cubes. How many of the cubes will have paint on:

   (a) One surface?
   (b) Two surfaces?
   (c) Three surfaces?

147. In a small town of 1000 homes, 15% have unlisted telephone numbers and 20% do not have a telephone number at all. If you select 500 numbers from the telephone directory at random, how many of those homes in that town will be unlisted?

148. Where will the symbols +, −, x and ÷ go if they are used once only to replace the question marks in the following, and what is the highest possible whole number answer?

$$4 \; ? \; 2 \; ? \; 5 \; ? \; 4 \; ? \; 9 \; =$$

149. Where will the symbols +, −, x and ÷ go if they are used once only to replace the question marks in the following, and what is the highest possible answer?

$$4 \; ? \; 5 \; ? \; 6 \; ? \; 3 \; ? \; 7 \; =$$

THE NUMBER JUMP

150. You throw three darts at this strange dartboard. How many ways are there to score 50 without a miss and no set of three numbers occurring in a different order?

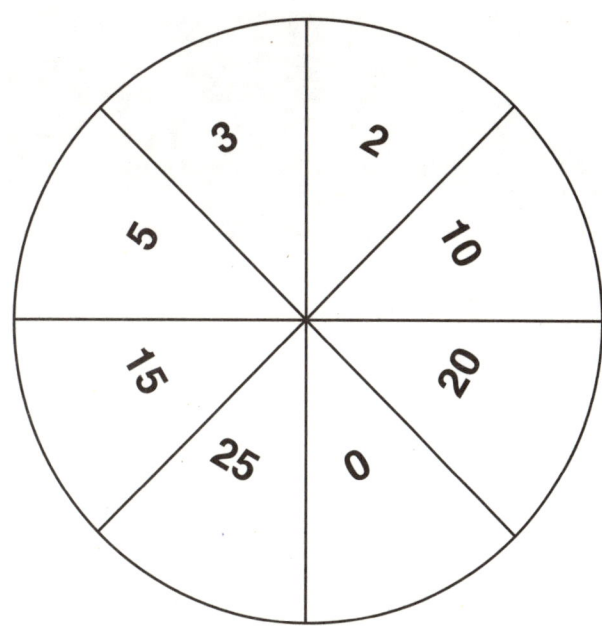

151. A car is going at 45 mph and is being followed by another car going at 40 mph. If the first car stops after 165m, how long will it take for the second car to catch up?

152. Can you determine what number should replace the question marks?

2	6	7	9	1				6	1	4	3	8				4	0	3	3	5		
8	0	2	7	6	D	F	A	9	4	4	2	3	B	I	H	?	?	?	?	?	G	C	E
5	3	0	2	4				3	2	6	8	7				1	9	7	8	1		

ZONE 2

ANSWERS

OBSTACLE 1

1. Player 2.
2. Player 3.
3. Player 6.
4. Player 3.
5. Players 1, 2 and 6.
6. Players 1, 2, 4 and 6.
7. 21.
8. 51.

OBSTACLE 2

9. 50.
10. 20.
11. 1280.
12. 1170.

OBSTACLE 3

13. ☐ = 3   △ = 5   ○ = 2   ○ = 7   ◉ = 4   ★ = 1   ■ = 6

ZONE 2

OBSTACLE 4

14. 66. Two previous numbers added.
15. 154. (n + 3) x 2.
16. 9, 20. Two series + 3, + 4, + 5, etc., and + 2 each time.
17. 51. (2n – 3).
18. –49. (2n – 15).
19. 70. (2n – 1^2), (2n – 2^2), etc.
20. 343. (n x previous n) ÷ 2.

OBSTACLE 5

21. 2. (A x B) – (D x E) = C
22. 6. (BC) + A = DE
23. 5. (Top row – 3rd row) + 2nd row = 4th row.

OBSTACLE 6

24. 97. Position of hands (not time) with hour hand, first, expressed as a sum.
113 – 16 = 97.
Others are: 51 + 123 = 174, 911 + 82 = 993.

25. 36. Position of hands (not time), expressed as minute hand – hour hand, then do sum.
(2 – 11) [–9] x (8 – 12) [–4] = 36.
Others are: (12 – 3)[9] x (7 – 5) [2] = 18, (6 – 2) [4] x (8 – 1) [7] = 28.

26. 16. Sum of segment values of shaded parts.

27. 216. Position of hands (not time), added together, then do sum.
(3 + 9) [12] x (12 + 6) [18] = 216.
Others are: (12 + 6) [18] + (6 + 3) [9] = 27, (12 + 9) [21] – (9 + 6)[15] = 5.

OBSTACLE 7

28. Move clockwise by the number of letters in the written number.

5		3
1		6

THE NUMBER JUMP

ZONE 2

THE NUMBER JUMP

29.

	21	
15		34
	22	

Move clockwise by the given number minus 1.

30.

17		6
9		3

Move clockwise by the given number plus 1.

OBSTACLE 8

31. 2. Make sums: First 2 digits − Second 2 digits, then First − Second.

32. 280. First digit x Fourth digit = First and Fourth digits, Second digit x Third digit = Second and Third digits.

33. 28. First digit x Second digit = First and Second digits, and Third digit x Fourth digit = Third and Fourth Digits.

OBSTACLE 9

34.

8	7	6	8	7	12	9	1
7	12	7	6	4	3	2	14
8	9	7	8	5	7	11	1
8	8	10	7	6	16	10	1
4	9	13	4	12	2	15	6
8	5	2	2	4	9	8	15
6	9	8	14	14	8	2	1
9	6	10	5	12	1	5	17

35.

5	7	8	15	4	7	5	6
11	6	9	8	16	12	10	10
7	12	10	12	3	11	6	8
6	7	2	5	7	7	15	10
12	15	10	8	5	12	8	7
6	7	11	13	9	6	9	6
9	8	10	6	8	8	1	2
3	6	4	10	10	10	15	15

Answers

ZONE 2

OBSTACLE 10

36. 40.

4	5	12	13
3	6	11	14
2	7	10	15
1	8	9	16

37. 36.

16	9	8	1
15	10	7	2
14	11	6	3
13	12	5	4

38. 41. The grid values are the same as for answer 37.

OBSTACLE 11

39. 37. (Top left + Top right) − (Bottom left + Bottom right).
40. 156. (Top left x Bottom right) + (Bottom left x Top right).
41. 54. (Top left x Bottom left) − (Top right x Bottom right).
42. 12. (Bottom left x Bottom right) − (Top left + Top right).
43. 68. (Top left^2 − Bottom right) + (Bottom left^2 − Top right).
44. 9. (Top left x Top right + Bottom left) ÷ Bottom right.
45. 126. (Top left + Top right + Bottom left) − Bottom right.
46. 960. (Top left x Top right x Bottom left) ÷ Bottom right.
47. 51. (Top left x Bottom right^2) − (Top right x Bottom left).
48. 114. Top left + Top right + Bottom left − Bottom right.

OBSTACLE 12

49. 17—19—22—24—28—20 = 130
50. 17—19—22—28—25—20 = 131
17—23—22—24—25—20 = 131
51. 140. 17—24—26—28—25—20
52. 127. 17—19—22—24—25—20
53. 2 ways: 17—24—26—24—25—20
17—23—22—26—28—20

The Number Jump

ZONE 2

THE NUMBER JUMP

OBSTACLE 13

54. 35—34—34—34—35—34—10
55. 35—32—29—28—37—33—10
  35—30—29—35—32—33—10
56. 219. 35—34—34—35—37—34—10
57. 202. 35—30—29—28—37—33—10
58. 4 ways: 35—32—29—35—37—33—10
  35—30—34—35—32—35—10
  35—33—32—34—32—35—10
  35—33—32—32—35—34—10

OBSTACLE 14

59. 29. Black = 7; White = 3; Shaded = 9.
60. 25. Black = 4; White = 5; Shaded = 6.
61. 25. Black = 5; White = 2; Shaded = 8.
62. 45. Black = 3; White = 8; Shaded = 13.
63. 17. Black = 4; White = 7; Shaded = 2.
64. 20. Black = 5; White = 3; Shaded = 4.
65. 16. Black = 5; White = 2; Shaded = 2.
66. 21. Black = 1; White = 6; Shaded = 7.
67. 47. Black = 0.8; White = 12.8; Shaded = 7.8.
68. 36. Black = 4; White = 3; Shaded = 8.

OBSTACLE 15

69. 26.
70. 36.
71. 34.
72. D4 = 70.
73. 16.
74. 4. (A6, B6).
75. ⊤ = 8   ● = 20
76. A2, C1, D6.
77. △ = 16   ⊙ = 24   ★ = 10
78. 102. D3.
79. 89.
80. 20. F6
81. 73.
82. Two, C5 and D5.

	A	B	C	D	E	F
1	28	28	32	26	16	8
2	32	●	46	46	⊤	16
3	36	44	□	64	42	34
4	26	⊤	56	54	□	40
5	16	16	34	48	●	36
6	4	4	22	32	28	28

	A	B	C	D	E	F
1	△	46	54	54	49	24
2	33	58	★	△	△	36
3	37	62	⊙	102	73	48
4	41	69	89	89	⊙	48
5	36	⊙	64	64	52	32
6	24	32	52	△	28	20

Answers

ZONE 2

THE NUMBER JUMP

OBSTACLE 16

(In answers 83–102, n = previous number)

83. 35. (n + 3), (n + 6), (n + 9), etc.
84. 94. (2n + 3), (2n + 6), (2n + 9), etc.
85. 1125. Multiply the previous two numbers.
86. 666. ($n^2 - 10$).
87. −25. (2n − 9).
88. 104. (3n − 1), (3n − 2), (3n − 3), (3n − 4), etc.
89. 360. (n x 5), (n x 4), (n x 3), etc.
90. 9. ($3n + 0^2$), ($2n + 1^2$), ($n + 2^2$), ($0 + 3^2$).
91. −37. (3n − 7).
92. −61. (27 − 2n).
93. 78. (2n − 5), (2n − 10), (2n − 15), (2n − 20).
94. 1280. −1(n + 1), −2(2n + 2), −3(3n + 3), −4(4n + 4).
95. 841. (7n − 6), (6n − 5), (5n − 4), (4n − 3).
96. 58. n + 11.
97. 130. (3n − 17).
98. 33. (n + 4), (n + 6), (n + 8), (n + 10).
99. 223. (3n − 5), (3n − 4), (3n − 3), (3n − 2).
100. −9. 2n − 7.
101. 116. $n^2 - 5$.
102. −5³⁄₅. (n − 2) ÷ 2, (n − 4) ÷ 2, (n − 6) ÷ 2, (n − 8) ÷ 2.

OBSTACLE 17

103. 120. Sum of left x sum of right.
104. −18. (Left numbers multiplied) − (right numbers multiplied).
105. 10. ((Outside top x outside bottom) − Inside). Left side − right side.
106. 360. All digits multiplied.
107. 82. (Bottom left x Top right) + Top left + Bottom right.
108. 100. (Bottom left x Bottom right) + Top left + Top right.

OBSTACLE 18

109. A6, C5, G6.
110. D2.
111. 12.
112. 117, occurs 3 times.
113. 91, G1.
114. E4.
115. None.
116. None.

Answers

ZONE 2

THE NUMBER JUMP

OBSTACLE 19

117. 175. (Window + Window) x Door.
118. 42. (Left window x Right window) – Door.
119. 71. (Left window x Door) + Right window.
120. 60. (Right window – Door) x Left window.
121. 93. Right window² – Left window² – Door.
122. 153. Door² – (Left window + Right window).

OBSTACLE 20

123. 48.
124. 64.
125. 8.
126. 32
127. 16.
128. 2.5.
129. 9.
130. 10.
131. 0.3.
132. 7.
133. Upside down on a calculator 0.37 reads: LEO.
134. 1 and 7.
135. None, it was full already.
136. 301.
137. 41312432 or 23421314.
138. He will have had seven wins and one loss in any order.
139. 2.

OBSTACLE 21

140. 3. Opposite segments total 30.
141. 25. (a x b) – c = d.
142. 18. Outside pair added = opposite one inside.

Answers

66

ZONE 2

OBSTACLE 22

143. Alan $26.50, & Brenda $15.50.
144. 13 of each 1c, 5c, 50c, 100c.
145. 207.
146. a) 1176.
b) 168.
c) 8.
147. None, only listed numbers will be in the directory!
148. 27. Divide, plus, minus, multiply.
149. 26.6. Divide, plus, minus, multiply.
150. 5.
151. 27 minutes & 30 seconds.
152. 60851. Top row + bottom row + letter values = middle row.

Scoring System

Do you get "Promoted" or "Busted"?

Promotion Criteria (See page 21):

Under 80	Demoted one rank.
81 - 100	No promotion.
101 - 130	Promoted one rank.
131 +	Promoted two ranks.

Age Bonus Points

Age in years	10	10.5	11	11.5	12	12.5	13	13.5	14	14.5	15	15.5
Bonus Points	50	45	40	35	30	25	20	16	14	12	8	4

Scoring System

ZONE ③

THE WORD CLIMB

Keep a firm grip and haul yourself up to find 110 hidden meanings, letters and words.

OBSTACLE 1 In each line below match the first given word with the word that is closest in meaning, and record your answer on the answer sheet.

		A	B	C	D	E
1.	RESCUE	Retrieve	Liberate	Salvage	Redeem	Help
2.	PROTESTOR	Rebel	Dissenter	Demonstrator	Marcher	Speaker
3.	AGGRAVATE	Anger	Insult	Enrage	Provoke	Instigate
4.	ETIQUETTE	Custom	Courtesies	Example	Manners	Protocol
5.	INVOLVEMENT	Participation	Concern	Responsibility	Implication	Association
6.	HERMIT	Solitaire	Recluse	Monk	Loner	Hoarder
7.	HASSLE	Problem	Nuisance	Worry	Bother	Trouble
8.	FICTIONAL	Legendary	Invention	Informal	Genuine	Imaginary
9.	EQUIVALENT	Alike	Twin	Equal	Even	Similar
10.	FASCINATE	Catch	Charm	Captivate	Occupy	Win
11.	THRIVING	Fit	Strong	Wholesome	Flourishing	Nourishing
12.	CONFIDE	Entrust	Limit	Secret	Disclose	Speak
13.	WANDER	Saunter	Stray	Veer	Drift	Depart
14.	NOURISHING	Good	Wholesome	Healthy	Improving	Worthy
15.	ESTIMATE	Guess	Roughly	Calculate	Close	Nearly
16.	THANKLESS	Unprofitable	Useless	Ungrateful	Worthless	Unsatisfying
17.	TRADITIONAL	Fixed	Accustomed	Old	Usual	Age-long
18.	APPREHENSION	Distrust	Misgiving	Threat	Wariness	Hunch
19.	AMAZE	Bewilder	Confuse	Astonish	Startle	Stagger
20.	PROFIT	Earnings	Interest	Revenue	Gain	Value

Answers on page 72

68

ZONE 3

OBSTACLE 2   Rearrange the letters given and make as many words as you can that use all of the letters. At least three words are possible from each group.

21.	A E G I L N R Y		22.	A E E H R T W
23.	E N O R S W		24.	C E I R R S T T
25.	B D E N O R S U		26.	A E G I L L S T
27.	A C D E I L M S		28.	A C H N S T
29.	A C E E R R S T		30.	E H I R T W
31.	E E L R S T W		32.	D E E R S T
33.	A D E E R R S T		34.	A C E L P R
35.	A D E L P		36.	B E E O R S V
37.	A E E N R S T		38.	A E L M N Y
39.	D E L M O R S		40.	D E G L N O

OBSTACLE 3   In each of the following groups of words a hidden common connection is present. Can you identify the connection?

41.	NARROWLY	TRAILER	GULLIBLE	JAYWALKING
42.	MARIGOLDS	JADEDNESS	EPISCOPAL	CHAMBER
43.	DISEASE	BETIDE	UNWAVERING	THREEFOLD
44.	CHROME	CORNICE	CLIMATE	BONNIEST
45.	BARNACLE	CHUTNEY	CRUSHED	CONTENTED
46.	COOKING	SHOOTER	MICROWAVE	ACRYLIC
47.	NARROWLY	GLANCED	HOAXERS	BURGUNDY
48.	ISSUE	SKIMPY	PAMPHLET	BANNER
49.	COMBATING	APPROXIMATE	OPERATE	PIGMENT
50.	CUSTARD	RISKY	HONEYMOON	MISUNDERSTAND

OBSTACLE 4   When each of the following words is rearranged, one group of letters can be used to prefix the others to form longer words. Which word is used as the prefix and what does it become?

	A	B	C	D
51.	RILE	COTS	MUSE	STILE
52.	SHORE	DIE	DUST	TEN
53.	FEATS	LOPE	RYE	BANE
54.	DENT	SON	LYRE	REED

Answers on pages 72 & 73

ZONE 3

55.	MAD	DEN	SAGE	LESS
56.	TOP	MOOR	EAT	LESS
57.	RED	AND	LEG	RIDE
58.	EMIT	BLEAT	STILE	RILE
59.	SHORE	HOSE	FILES	SHELF
60.	GIN	CEDES	COLA	FILED

OBSTACLE 5 Rearrange the following to form five connected words or names. What are they?

61.	TOUGHDUN	FACETIKUR	BRAGGRINDEE	CAJPALKF	CRANOOMA
62.	HETCS	RESSERD	STEETE	BALET	DAWBRORE
63.	DIALDOFF	PRONDOWS	FUNERSLOW	CHISUFA	GONEIBA
64.	OCAIR	ELOUS	HTAENS	HAGABDD	GANKKOB
65.	TREAKA	FOLG	BYGUR	DUOJ	TINDBONAM
66.	WOIBE	SORS	SCONKAJ	STRANDISE	PLESREY
67.	NARI	LICHE	RUGAPAYA	LISARE	HOLDALN
68.	PORIPNEPE	SORTITO	ZAPIZ	MAISAL	PATAS
69.	GUTTSTART	MORDDNUT	BRINLE	NOBN	GRELEBIDEH
70.	CREMRUIT	NINACNOM	NACEYEN	MUNCI	GRONEAO

OBSTACLE 6 Add the vowels in the following groups of letters to form five words, one of which does not belong with the others. Which word is the odd one out?

71.	GLV	HT	SCRF	SHWL	BRCLT
72.	DNM	KHK	NYLN	SLK	WL
73.	PLT	DSH	SCR	CHN	BKR
74.	BNGLW	FLT	HS	GRDN	MSNTT
75.	QRTT	GTR	ZTHR	TRMBN	PN
76.	DNCR	GRCR	SLR	DRVR	STDNT
77.	BLTMR	RZN	PHNX	CHCG	HSTN
78.	VDK	BRBN	GRVY	DVCT	BRNDY
79.	DMNND	LLGR	FRTSSM	HRPSCHRD	CRSCND
80.	MRYLND	NDN	NVD	GRG	BSTN

Answers on pages 73 & 74

ZONE 3

OBSTACLE 7   Join the letters of the given words to form a single word using all of the letters.

81.	PEER	+	DAMP	82.	CLUE	+	PAIR
83.	MEAL	+	DIVE	84.	CURE	+	MAIN
85.	HALL	+	SEES	86.	SCENE	+	TEN
87.	RATE	+	RUSE	88.	ENSURE	+	DEBT
89.	WALL	+	FREE	90.	CANE	+	TERN

OBSTACLE 8   Each of the following words has the prefix missing. The prefix on each question is the same for all of the words in that question. Can you find the prefixes for the following?

91.	_ _ _ DOWY	_ _ _ KING	_ _ _ LLOT	_ _ _ RING
92.	_ _ _ ITAN	_ _ _ PLES	_ _ _ POSE	_ _ _ SUIT
93.	_ _ _ ADOR	_ _ _ CHED	_ _ _ INEE	_ _ _ URED
94.	_ _ _ EVER	_ _ _ DDLE	_ _ _ MACE	_ _ _ PPER
95.	_ _ _ AWAY	_ _ _ MING	_ _ _ THER	_ _ _ MERS

OBSTACLE 9   For each word shown write another word with the same meaning beginning with the letter "C".

96.	PSYCHIC	97.	ATROCITY
98.	ACCURATE	99.	OPPOSE
100.	INFORMAL	101.	PUNISH
102.	SLINGSHOT	103.	INEXPENSIVE
104.	ANGEL	105.	INFANT

OBSTACLE 10   In each question can you underline the two words that are nearest in meaning?

	A	B	C	D	E
106.	Encourage	Indicate	Assure	Suggest	Promise
107.	Assembly	Direction	Presentation	Construction	Preparation
108.	Early	Instant	Alert	Immediate	Efficient
109.	Prospect	Verification	Proof	Trial	Demonstration
110.	Skill	Professional	Cleverness	Readiness	Talent

Answers on pages 74 & 75

ZONE 3

ANSWERS

OBSTACLE 1

1.	C.	2.	B.
3.	D.	4.	D.
5.	A.	6.	B.
7.	D.	8.	E.
9.	C	10.	C.
11.	D.	12.	A.
13.	D.	14.	B.
15.	C.	16.	C.
17.	B.	18.	D.
19.	C.	20.	D.

OBSTACLE 2

21.	Relaying, Layering, Yearling.	22.	Wreathe, Weather, Whereat.
23.	Owners, Worsen, Rowens.	24.	Stricter, Critters, Restrict.
25.	Bounders, Rebounds, Suborned.	26.	Legalist, Stillage, Tillages.
27.	Decimals, Medicals, Declaims.	28.	Stanch, Snatch, Chants.
29.	Retraces, Terraces, Caterers.	30.	Whiter, Wither, Writhe.
31.	Wrestle, Swelter, Welters.	32.	Rested, Desert, Deters.
33.	Serrated, Treaders, Retreads.	34.	Parcel, Carpel, Placer.
35.	Paled, Pedal, Plead.	36.	Observe, Obverse, Verbose.
37.	Earnest, Eastern, Nearest.	38.	Namely, Meanly, Laymen.
39.	Remolds, Smolder, Molders.	40.	Dongle, Golden, Longed.

ZONE 3

OBSTACLE 3

41. Owl, Rail, Gull, Jay.
42. Gold, Jade, Opal, Amber.
43. Sea, Tide, Wave, Reef.
44. Rome, Nice, Lima, Bonn.
45. Barn, Hut, Shed, Tent.
46. Coo, Hoot, Crow, Cry.
47. Arrow, Lance, Axe, Gun.
48. Sue, Kim, Pam, Anne (or Ann).
49. Bat, Ox, Rat, Pig.
50. Star, Sky, Moon, Sun.

OBSTACLE 4

51. Cost, which makes Costlier, Costumes, Costliest.
52. Stud, which makes Studhorse, Studied, Student.
53. Bean, which makes Beanfeast, Beanpole, Beanery.
54. Tend, which makes Tendons, Tenderly, Tendered.
55. Dam, which makes Damned, Damages, Damsels.
56. Tea, which makes Teapot, Tearoom, Teasels.
57. Dan, which makes Dander, Dangle, Dandier.
58. Time, which makes Timetable, Timelist, Timelier.
59. Horse, which makes Horseshoe, Horseflies, Horseflesh.
60. Coal, which makes Coaling, Coalesced, Coalfield.

OBSTACLE 5

61. Doughnut, Fruitcake, Gingerbread, Flapjack, Macaroon.
62. Chest, Dresser, Settee, Table, Wardrobe.
63. Daffodil, Snowdrop, Sunflower, Fuchsia, Begonia.
64. Cairo, Seoul, Athens, Baghdad, Bangkok.
65. Karate, Golf, Rugby, Judo, Badminton.
66. Bowie, Ross, Jackson, Streisand, Presley.
67. Iran, Chile, Paraguay, Israel, Holland.
68. Pepperoni, Risotto, Pizza, Salami, Pasta.
69. Stuttgart, Dortmund, Berlin, Bonn, Heidelberg.
70. Turmeric, Cinnamon, Cayenne, Cumin, Oregano.

Answers

ZONE 3

OBSTACLE 6

71. Bracelet. Others are Glove, Hat, Scarf, Shawl.
72. Khaki. Others are Denim, Nylon, Silk, Wool.
73. China. Others are Plate, Dish, Saucer, Beaker.
74. Garden. Others are Bungalow, Flat, House, Maisonette.
75. Quartet. Others are Guitar, Zither, Trombone, Piano.
76. Student. Others are Dancer, Grocer, Sailor, Driver.
77. Arizona. Others are Baltimore, Phoenix, Chicago, Houston.
78. Gravy. Others are Vodka, Bourbon, Advocaat, Brandy.
79. Harpsichord. Others are Diminuendo, Allegro, Fortissimo, Crescendo.
80. Boston. Others are Maryland, Indiana, Nevada, Georgia.

OBSTACLE 7

81. Pampered.
82. Peculiar.
83. Medieval.
84. Manicure.
85. Seashell.
86. Sentence.
87. Treasure.
88. Debentures.
89. Farewell.
90. Entrance.

OBSTACLE 8

91. Sha.
92. Pur.
93. Mat.
94. Gri.
95. Far.

OBSTACLE 9

96. Clairvoyant.
97. Cruelty.
98. Correct.
99. Counter.
100. Casual.
101. Chastise.
102. Catapult.
103. Cheap.
104. Cherub.
105. Child.

Answers

ZONE 3

OBSTACLE 10

106. C & E.
107. A & D.
108. B & D.
109. B & C.
110. A & E.

Scoring System

Is Your Progress Slow?

Promotion Criteria (See page 21):

Under 50 :	*"Are you sure you should be in the Army?"* Demoted one rank.
51 - 70	*"Sorry, you must try harder."* No promotion.
71 - 90	*"Training is going well."* Promoted one rank.
91 +	*"Real promise shown."* Promoted two ranks.

AGE BONUS POINTS

Age in Years	10	10.5	11	11.5	12	12.5	13	13.5	14	14.5	15	15.5
Bonus Points	30	25	20	18	17	16	14	12	10	8	6	3

ZONE 4

You only have a few minutes to memorize vital information. If you get forgetful now your score will plummet.

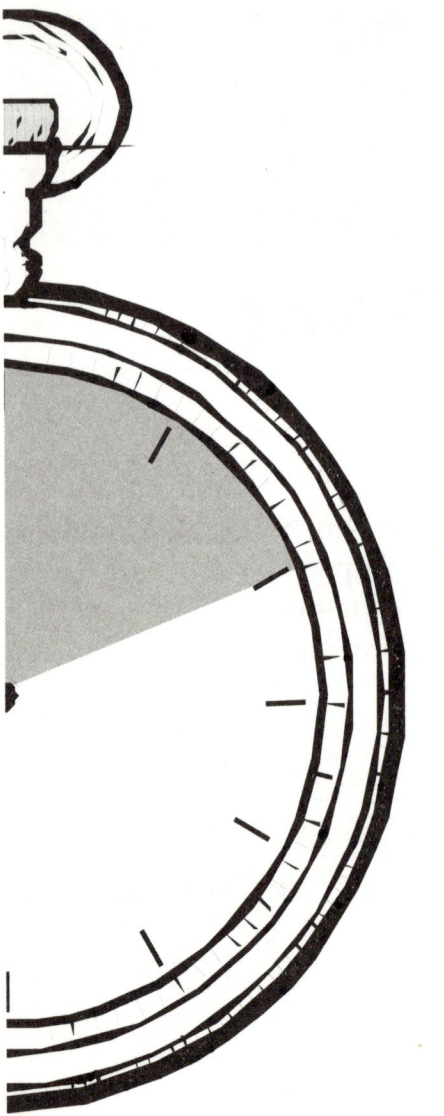

MEMORY TEST 1

Study the next page of property particulars for 2 minutes, then begin the test on the next page.

ONCE THE TEST HAS STARTED YOU
MUST NOT LOOK BACK

Set the clock and begin

Time allowed for this test
10 MINUTES

THE MEMORY TESTS

PROPERTY FOR SALE

The Old Stone House Manor,
Farmhouse Lane,
Hookey,
Worcestershire.

An eye-catching three-storey detached manor house is being sold on the outskirts of Hookey. The property dates back to Elizabethan times and over the last 10 years has been restored considerably, but retains its period atmosphere (including ceiling beams). The property is south-facing with magnificent views over the River Dean and picturesque woodland beyond. There is easy access to the A454 and the B2314.

The property is equipped with gas-fired central heating, double-glazing and a security system.

Offers around **£235,000** are being invited for this freehold home.

The three-storey property has a living room, drawing room, sitting room, breakfast kitchen, utility room, cloakroom and storeroom on the ground floor. On the first floor there are 4 bedrooms (2 with en-suites), and the main bathroom has a spa corner-bath, shower and adjoining dressing room. On the second floor you will find three more bedrooms together with a large games room. There is a large double garage joined on to the property, which is adequate to park three cars.

The property is surrounded by a courtyard, which is well established with a wide variety of shrubs and trees. The borders are well stocked and there is a vegetable patch with potatoes, carrots, lettuces, onions, garlic and broad beans. The property can be viewed by contacting the owners.

ZONE 4

THE MEMORY TESTS

1. What is the name of the house?
2. In what town is it situated?
3. Is it in Warwickshire or Worcestershire?
4. How many storeys does the property have?
5. In what part of Hookey will you find the property?
6. In what period was the house built?
7. Does the property have ceiling beams?
8. What is the asking price of the property?
9. Should you contact the agents to view the property?
10. How many bedrooms does the property have?
11. What room adjoins the main bathroom?
12. Does the bathroom have a power shower?
13. How many bedrooms are on the second floor?
14. What two main roads are within easy access to the property?
15. What river can be viewed from the property?
16. Does the property have double-glazing or secondary glazing?
17. Where will you find the games room?
18. What vegetables can be found on the vegetable patch?
19. Is there an orchard?
20. How many cars can you park in the garage?
21. Is the garage joined on to the property?
22. Does the property face south-east?
23. Apart from the river, what else can be viewed from the property?
24. Is there a drawing room on the ground floor?
25. Are there two bedrooms or three bedrooms with en-suites?

ZONE 4

THE MEMORY TESTS

1. _____
2. _____
3. _____
4. _____
5. _____
6. _____
7. _____
8. _____
9. _____
10. _____
11. _____
12. _____
13. _____
14. _____
15. _____
16. _____
17. _____
18. _____
19. _____
20. _____
21. _____
22. _____
23. _____
24. _____
25. _____

Answers on page 104

ZONE 4

OBSTACLE 2

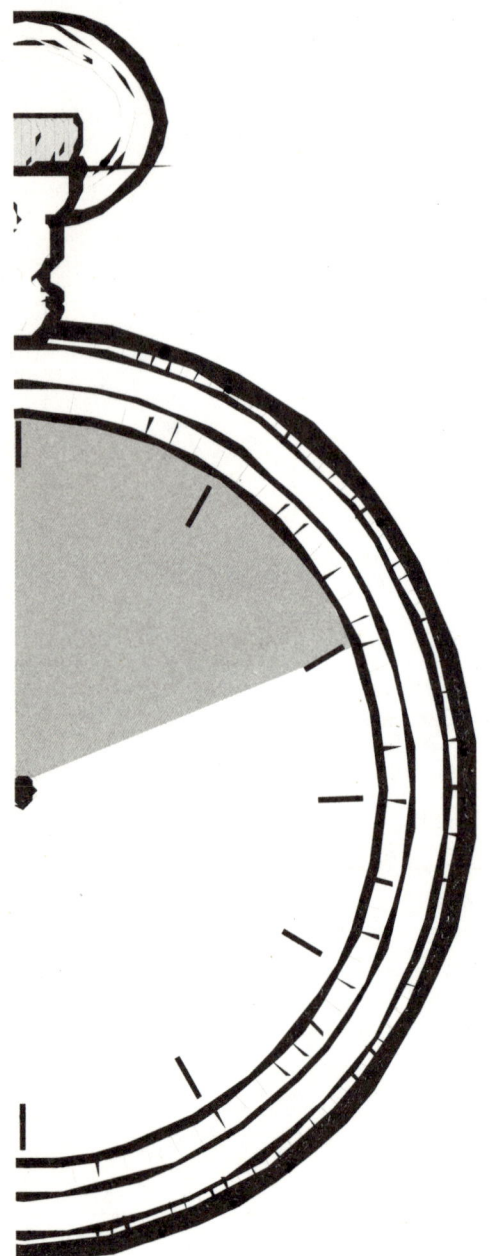

MEMORY TEST 2

Study the crossword opposite for 2 minutes, then begin the test on the next page. The crossword is made up of words for fruits, vegetables and animals.

ONCE THE TEST HAS STARTED YOU MUST NOT LOOK BACK

Set the clock and begin

Time allowed for this test
10 MINUTES

ZONE 4

THE MEMORY TESTS

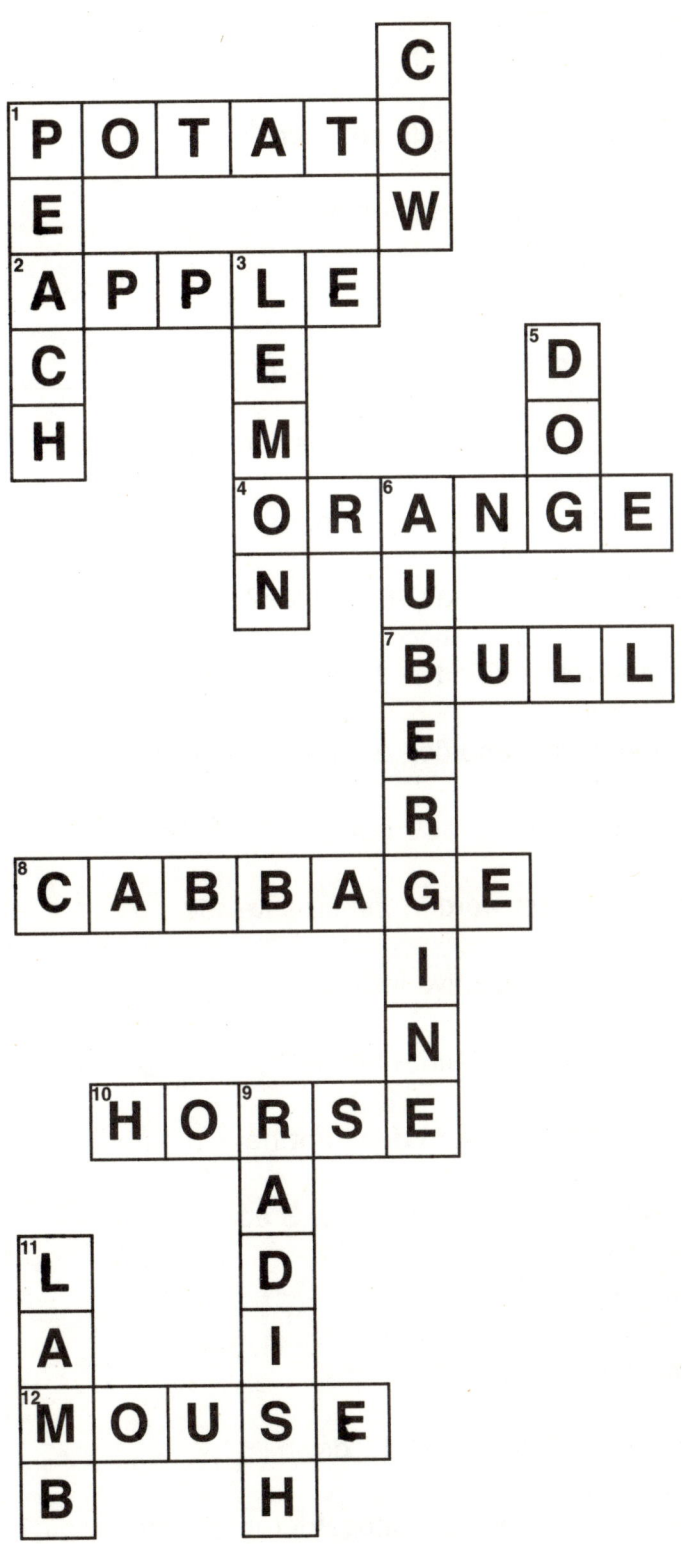

81

ZONE 4

1. How many types of fruit are there?
2. How many types of animals are there?
3. How many types of vegetables are there?
4. Is 3 down a fruit or vegetable?
5. Does cabbage go across the puzzle or down it?
6. What animal is at 5 down and runs through orange?
7. Is there an onion in the crossword?
8. Are there more fruits than vegetables?
9. What animal will you find at 12 across?
10. Is there more than one dog on the crossword?
11. What item will you find at 9 down?
12. What is the longest word in the crossword?
13. How many words have five letters?
14. How many words have three letters?
15. One item in the crossword does not have a number. Which is it?
16. Can apple be found at 2 across or 3 across?
17. Where will you find bull?
18. Where will you find carrot?
19. What animal will you find at 11 down?
20. How many words are there altogether in the crossword?

ZONE 4

THE MEMORY TESTS

1. _____
2. _____
3. _____
4. _____
5. _____
6. _____
7. _____
8. _____
9. _____
10. _____
11. _____
12. _____
13. _____
14. _____
15. _____
16. _____
17. _____
18. _____
19. _____
20. _____

Answers on page 104

ZONE 4

THE MEMORY TESTS

MEMORY TEST 3

Study the flight timetable opposite for 2 minutes, then begin the test on the next page.

ONCE THE TEST HAS STARTED YOU
MUST NOT LOOK BACK

Set the clock and begin

Time allowed for this test
10 MINUTES

ZONE 4

Study the timetable showing departure time, destination and airline.

DEPARTURE TIME	DESTINATION	AIRLINE
0630	PARIS	BRITISH AIRWAYS
0645	SPAIN	IBERIA
0705	MOMBASSA	MONARCH
0755	FLORIDA	VIRGIN ATLANTIC
0910	CYPRUS	DELTA
0945	IRELAND	AEROFLOT
1000	CHINA	CATHAY PACIFIC
1020	JAMAICA	OLYMPIC
1245	INDIA	KLM
1300	IRELAND	IBERIA
1345	AMSTERDAM	AEROFLOT

THE MEMORY TESTS

ZONE 4

THE MEMORY TESTS

1. How many flights are there altogether?

2. At what time is the first flight?

3. What is the destination of the flight that leaves at 09.45?

4. How many flights are there to Ireland?

5. What airline is the flight to Jamaica?

6. Which country are you flying to if you travel by Cathay Pacific?

7. What time does the flight to India leave?

8. Where would you be travelling to if you leave at 07.55 by Virgin Atlantic?

9. What time is the flight to Sydney?

10. What is the name of the airline that leaves at 12.45?

11. If you leave at 12.45, are you going to India or Ireland?

12. How many flights are there to India?

13. How many flights are there by Iberia Airlines?

14. What time is the last flight?

15. Where are you flying if you leave at 10.25?

16. Are there any flights by Aer Lingus?

17. What time is the flight to Spain?

18. If you are travelling to China, do you leave at 10.00 or 10.20?

19. Does the flight to Cyprus leave at 09.10 by Delta Airlines?

20. Does the flight to Jamaica leave at 10.10 by Olympic Airlines?

ZONE 4

THE MEMORY TESTS

1. _____
2. _____
3. _____
4. _____
5. _____
6. _____
7. _____
8. _____
9. _____
10. _____
11. _____
12. _____
13. _____
14. _____
15. _____
16. _____
17. _____
18. _____
19. _____
20. _____

Answers on page 104

ZONE ④

THE MEMORY TESTS

MEMORY TEST 4

Study the car park details opposite for 2 minutes, then begin the test on the next page.

ONCE THE TEST HAS STARTED YOU
MUST NOT LOOK BACK

Set the clock and begin

Time allowed for this test
10 MINUTES

ZONE 4

THE MEMORY TESTS

ST. MARY'S CAR PARK

Opening Times:	7.30 am
	to 6.30 pm

Car-parking prices:

Up to **1 hour**	$0.50
2 hours	$1.00
3 hours	$1.50
Over 3 hours	$2.30

1. | RED MINI | RED CORSA | WHITE FIESTA | SILVER AUDI | GREEN LAND-ROVER |

2. | | WHITE VAN | GOLD MERCEDES | RED CORSA | GREEN PEUGEOT |

3. | | BLACK ASTRA | BLACK ESCORT | BLACK BMW | YELLOW MGBT |

4. | YELLOW HONDA 600 | | | BLUE RANGE ROVER | RED PORSCHE | | |

89

ZONE 4

THE MEMORY TESTS

1. What was the name of the car park?
2. How many prices were listed on the price list?
3. How many rows of car parking spaces were there?
4. How many spaces were there altogether?
5. How many spaces were there on Row 4?
6. How many car parking spaces were unoccupied?
7. How many car parking spaces were unoccupied on Row 1?
8. How many cars were parked altogether?
9. How many red cars were there in the car park?
10. How many cream cars were there?
11. Which car was between the gold Mercedes and the green Peugeot?
12. Which car was parked in the middle of Row 1?
13. How many Corsas were there?
14. How many hours a day was the car park open?
15. What time did the car park close?
16. How many different makes of car were in the car park?
17. Was the only Escort red, white, green, blue or black?
18. Was the Range Rover green, blue or white?
19. You drive into the Car Park and go next to the Black Astra. Which row are you on?
20. What is the most popular shade of car?
21. How much does it cost you to park for 3½ hours?

ZONE 4

THE MEMORY TESTS

1. _____
2. _____
3. _____
4. _____
5. _____
6. _____
7. _____
8. _____
9. _____
10. _____
11. _____
12. _____
13. _____
14. _____
15. _____
16. _____
17. _____
18. _____
19. _____
20. _____
21. _____

Answers on page 104

ZONE ④

THE MEMORY TESTS

MEMORY TEST 5

Study the map opposite for 2 minutes, then begin the test on the next page.

ONCE THE TEST HAS STARTED YOU MUST NOT LOOK BACK

Set the clock and begin

Time allowed for this test
10 MINUTES

ZONE 4

THE MEMORY TESTS

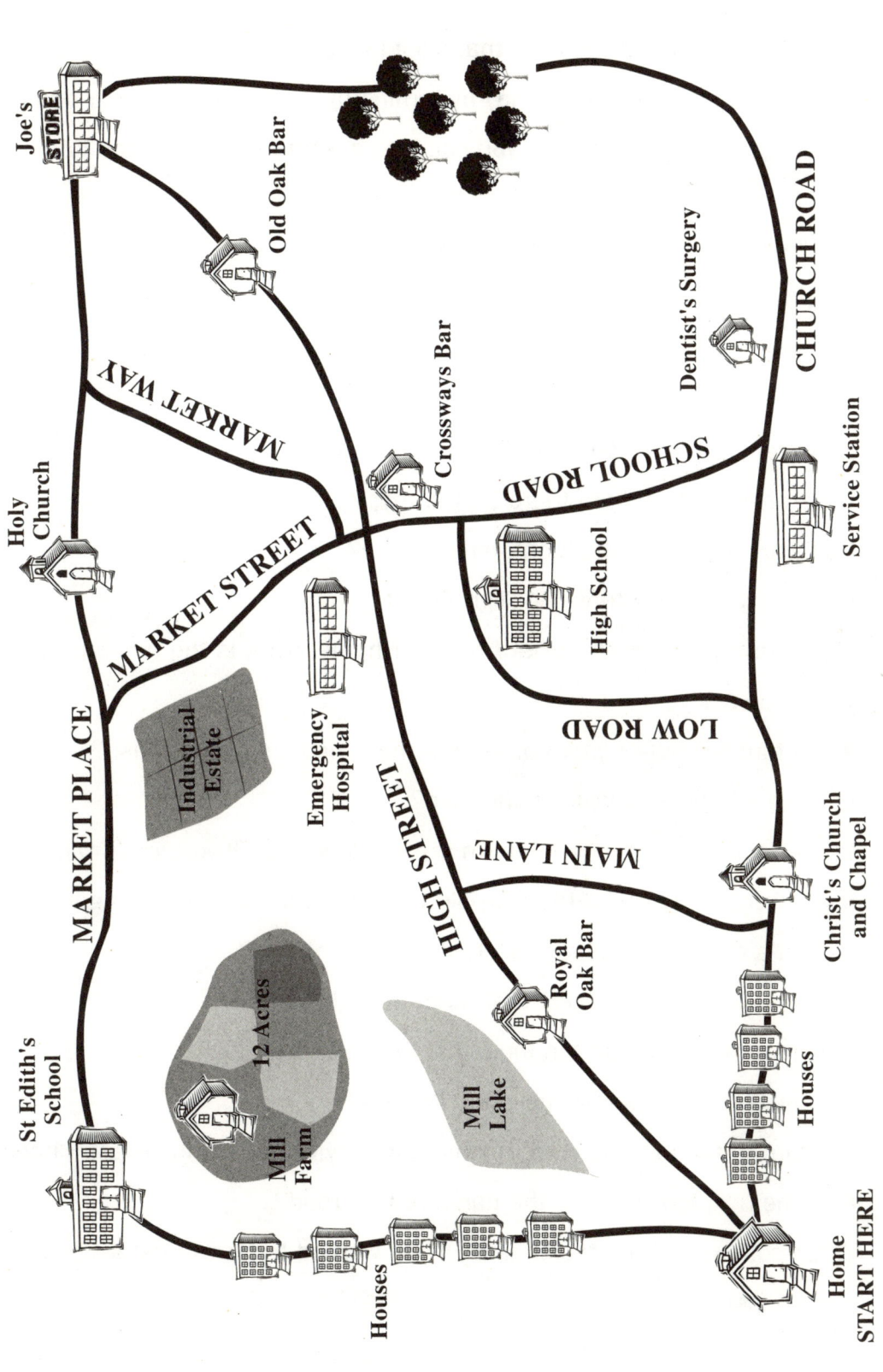

ZONE 4

THE MEMORY TESTS

1. What is the name of the road that would take you directly to Joe's store?
2. You decide to start your journey by turning right as you leave your home. Before you reach the church you come to a left turn. What is the name of that road?
3. On what road would you find the Royal Oak bar?
4. How many bars are there on the map?
5. Is there a dentist's surgery on the map?
6. What is the name of the farm on the map?
7. How many acres of land does the farm have?
8. How many churches are there on the map?
9. Can you name the school on Market Place?
10. How many bars are there on High Street?
11. If you travel along High Street from your home, what is the name of the third bar you come to?
12. If you turn left out of your home, how many houses do you pass?
13. Is there a pond or a lake on the map?
14. Which road would you travel down if you needed to fill your car's tank?
15. If you went along High Street, would you take a left or a right to get to the dentist's surgery when you reached the second bar?
16. Name one of the two roads that meet at High School?
17. How many units are on the Industrial Estate?
18. How many roads contain the word "Market"?
19. You turn to the right from your home, pass by Christ's Church and Chapel, and take the next left. What is the name of that road?
20. Which road would you travel along if you wanted to visit Christ's Church and Chapel?

ZONE 4

THE MEMORY TESTS

1. _____
2. _____
3. _____
4. _____
5. _____
6. _____
7. _____
8. _____
9. _____
10. _____
11. _____
12. _____
13. _____
14. _____
15. _____
16. _____
17. _____
18. _____
19. _____
20. _____

Answers on page 105

ZONE ④

THE MEMORY TESTS

MEMORY TEST 6

Study the street plan opposite for 2 minutes, then begin the test on the next page.

ONCE THE TEST HAS STARTED YOU
MUST NOT LOOK BACK

Set the clock and begin

Time allowed for this test
10 MINUTES

ZONE ④

THE MEMORY TESTS

LONGFORD HALL LANE

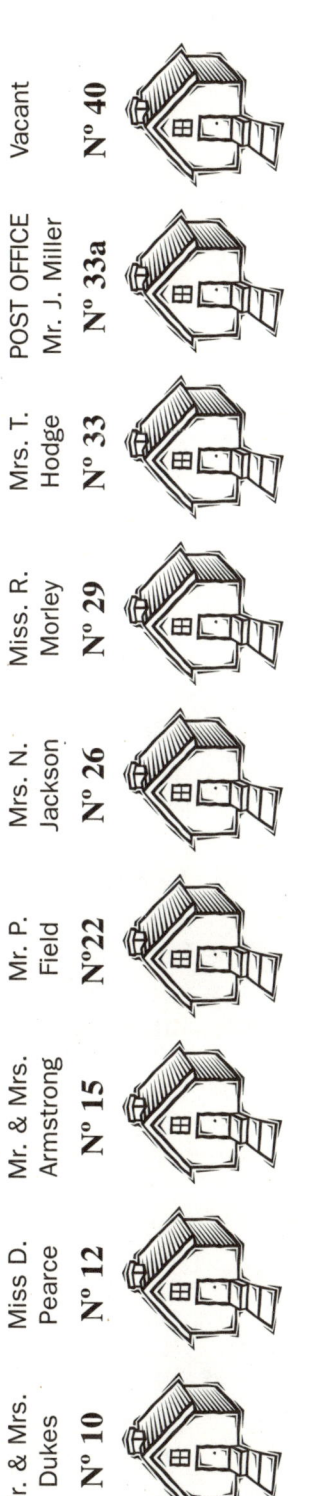

Nº 10	Mr. & Mrs. Dukes
Nº 12	Miss D. Pearce
Nº 15	Mr. & Mrs. Armstrong
Nº 22	Mr. P. Field
Nº 26	Mrs. N. Jackson
Nº 29	Miss. R. Morley
Nº 33	Mrs. T. Hodge
Nº 33a	POST OFFICE Mr. J. Miller
Nº 40	Vacant

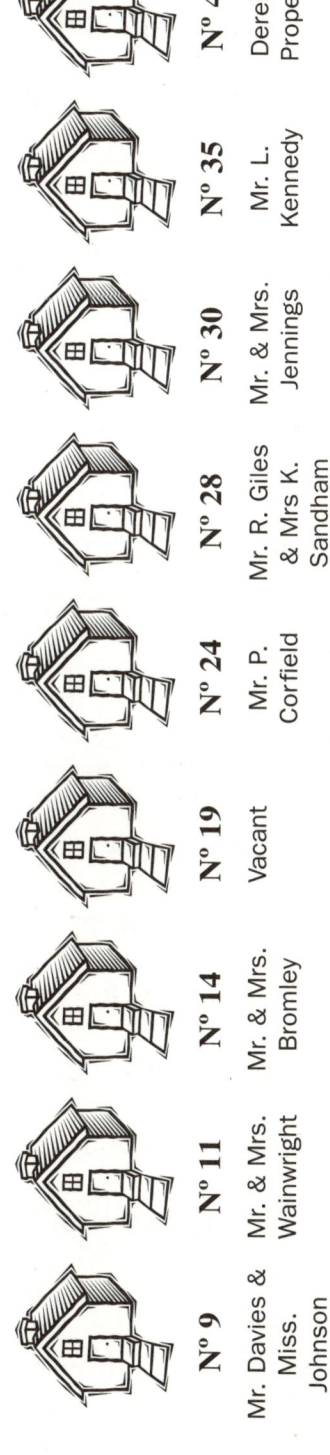

Nº 9	Mr. Davies & Miss. Johnson
Nº 11	Mr. & Mrs. Wainwright
Nº 14	Mr. & Mrs. Bromley
Nº 19	Vacant
Nº 24	Mr. P. Corfield
Nº 28	Mr. R. Giles & Mrs K. Sandham
Nº 30	Mr. & Mrs. Jennings
Nº 35	Mr. L. Kennedy
Nº 43	Derelict Property

97

ZONE 4

THE MEMORY TESTS

1. What is the name of the street?
2. How many houses are there altogether?
3. How many houses are occupied by men only?
4. How many houses are occupied by women only?
5. What is the name of the couple who occupy No. 10?
6. Who lives at No. 22?
7. Is house No. 40 vacant?
8. Is house No. 11 vacant?
9. Who occupies the Post Office?
10. Who lives between Mr. and Mrs. Bromley and Mr. P. Corfield?
11. Is Miss Johnson one of the occupiers of No. 9?
12. What is the initial of Miss Pearce who lives at No. 12?
13. Standing on the street, who lives to the left of the Post Office?
14. Does Mr. R. Giles occupy the same house as Miss. R. Morley?
15. Who lives with Mr. L. Kennedy?
16. What number is the house opposite No. 22?
17. How many houses are unoccupied?
18. At what number does Mrs. K. Sandham live?
19. What is the number of the derelict property?
20. Does Mr. P. Field occupy No. 22?

ZONE 4

THE MEMORY TESTS

1. _____
2. _____
3. _____
4. _____
5. _____
6. _____
7. _____
8. _____
9. _____
10. _____
11. _____
12. _____
13. _____
14. _____
15. _____
16. _____
17. _____
18. _____
19. _____
20. _____

Answers on page 105

ZONE ④

THE MEMORY TESTS

MEMORY TEST 7

Study the grid opposite for 3 minutes, then begin the test on the next page.

ONCE THE TEST HAS STARTED YOU
MUST NOT LOOK BACK

Set the clock and begin

Time allowed for this test
10 MINUTES

ZONE 4

THE MEMORY TESTS

	1	2	3	4	5	6	
	$	¶	Q	=	¶	Ó	A
	$	¶	2	4	Ó	Ó	B
	Ó	Z	4	$	$	$	C
	3	$	=	Ó	Q	3	D
	Q	Z	¶	$	Ó	¶	E
	¶	%	=	%	&	%	F

ZONE 4

1. What numbers go across the top of the page?
2. What letters go down the right side of the page?
3. What letter will you find in box 2C?
4. What symbol will you find in box 1A?
5. In order from the left, list the symbols that appear in row F.
6. Which symbol appears three times in row C?
7. How many boxes contain the symbol ¶?
8. Does a 4 or a $ follow Z in row C?
9. How many different numbers are there inside the table?
10. How many different letters are there inside the table?
11. In order from the top, list the symbols that appear in column 1.
12. In which row will you find three % symbols?
13. In which row will you find three $ symbols?
14. How many & symbols are in the grid?
15. What symbol can be found in box 1D?
16. Is there a Q or a $ in box 5D?
17. How many = symbols are there?
18. What letter comes before Z in row E?
19. Reading from the left, what is last symbol in row F?
20. How many of the letter Q are there?

ZONE 4

THE MEMORY TESTS

1. _____
2. _____
3. _____
4. _____
5. _____
6. _____
7. _____
8. _____
9. _____
10. _____
11. _____
12. _____
13. _____
14. _____
15. _____
16. _____
17. _____
18. _____
19. _____
20. _____

Answers on page 105

ZONE 4

ANSWERS

Memory Test 1

1. The Old Stone House Manor.
2. Hookey.
3. Worcestershire.
4. 3.
5. The outskirts.
6. Elizabethan.
7. Yes.
8. £235,000.
9. No.
10. 7
11. Dressing room.
12. No.
13. 3.
14. A454 and B2314.
15. River Dean.
16. Double-glazing.
17. Second floor.
18. Potatoes, Carrots, Onions, Lettuces, Garlic, Broad Beans.
19. No.
20. 3.
21. Yes.
22. No.
23. Woodland.
24. Yes.
25. 2.

Memory Test 2

1. 4.
2. 6.
3. 4.
4. Fruit.
5. Across.
6. Dog.
7. No.
8. The same.
9. Mouse.
10. No.
11. Radish.
12. Aubergine.
13. 5.
14. 2.
15. Cow.
16. 2 across.
17. 7 across.
18. You will not.
19. Lamb.
20. 14.

Memory Test 3

1. 11.
2. 06.30.
3. Ireland.
4. 2.
5. Olympic.
6. China.
7. 12.45.
8. Florida.
9. There is not one.
10. KLM.
11. India.
12. 1.
13. 2.
14. 13.45.
15. There is not a flight at 10.25.
16. No.
17. 06.45.
18. 10.00.
19. Yes.
20. No.

Memory Test 4

1. St. Mary's.
2. 4.
3. 4.
4. 22.
5. 7.
6. 6.
7. None.
8. 16.
9. 4.
10. None.
11. Red Corsa.
12. White Fiesta.
13. 2.
14. 11 hours.
15. 6.30 pm.
16. 14.
17. Black.
18. Blue.
19. Row 3.
20. Red.
21. $2.30.

ZONE 4

THE MEMORY TESTS

Memory Test 5

1. High Street.
2. Main Lane.
3. High Street.
4. 3.
5. Yes.
6. Mill Farm.
7. 12 Acres.
8. 2.
9. St. Edith's School.
10. 3.
11. Old Oak.
12. 5.
13. A lake.
14. Church Road.
15. Right.
16. Low Road/ School Road.
17. 8.
18. 3.
19. Low Road.
20. Church Road.

Memory Test 6

1. Longford Hall Lane.
2. 18.
3. 3.
4. 4.
5. Mr. and Mrs. Dukes.
6. Mr. P. Field.
7. Yes.
8. No.
9. Mr. J. Miller.
10. No-one.
11. Yes.
12. D.
13. Mrs. T. Hodge.
14. No.
15. No-one.
16. No. 19.
17. 3.
18. No. 28.
19. No. 43.
20. Yes.

Memory Test 7

1. 1, 2, 3, 4, 5 and 6.
2. A, B, C, D, E and F.
3. Z.
4. $.
5. ¶, %, =, %, &, %.
6. $.
7. 6.
8. 4.
9. 3.
10. 3. Ó, Z, Q.
11. $, $, Ó, 3, Q, ¶.
12. F.
13. C.
14. 1.
15. 3.
16. Q.
17. 3.
18. Q.
19. %.
20. 3.

Answers

ZONE 4

SCORING SYSTEM

This was to see if you could get into "Special Forces"

Promotion Criteria (See page 21):

Average Paper Scores

Less than 6	"*Suggest a new trade.*" Demoted one rank.
7 – 10	No progress.
11 – 14	Promoted one rank.
15 +	Promoted two ranks and selected for Special Forces.

AGE BONUS POINTS

AGE IN YEARS	10	10.5	11	11.5	12	12.5	13	13.5	14	14.5	15	15.5
BONUS POINTS	3	3	3	3	2	2	2	2	1	1	1	0

ZONE 5

The only way out of this section is to decipher 50 devious visual puzzles of logic and recognition.

THE SPATIAL LOGIC DODGE

OBSTACLE 1 Which of the following is the odd one out?

1.

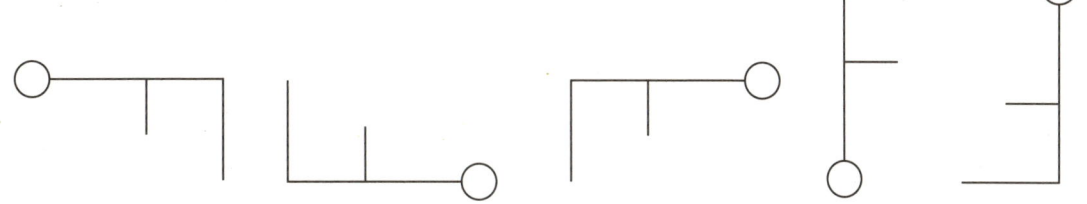

A B C D E

2.

A B C D E

3.

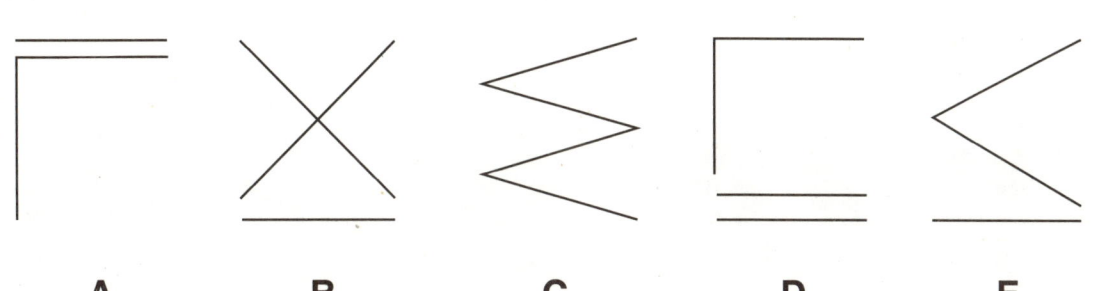

A B C D E

Answers on page 127

ZONE 5

THE SPATIAL LOGIC DODGE

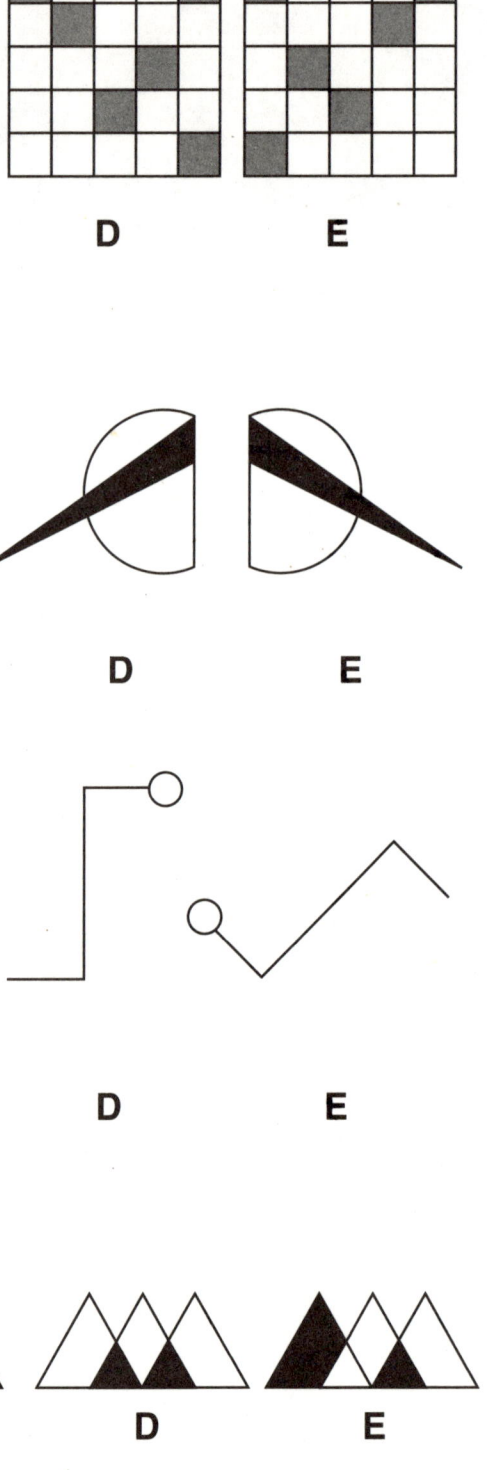

108 Answers on page 127

ZONE 5

THE SPATIAL LOGIC DODGE

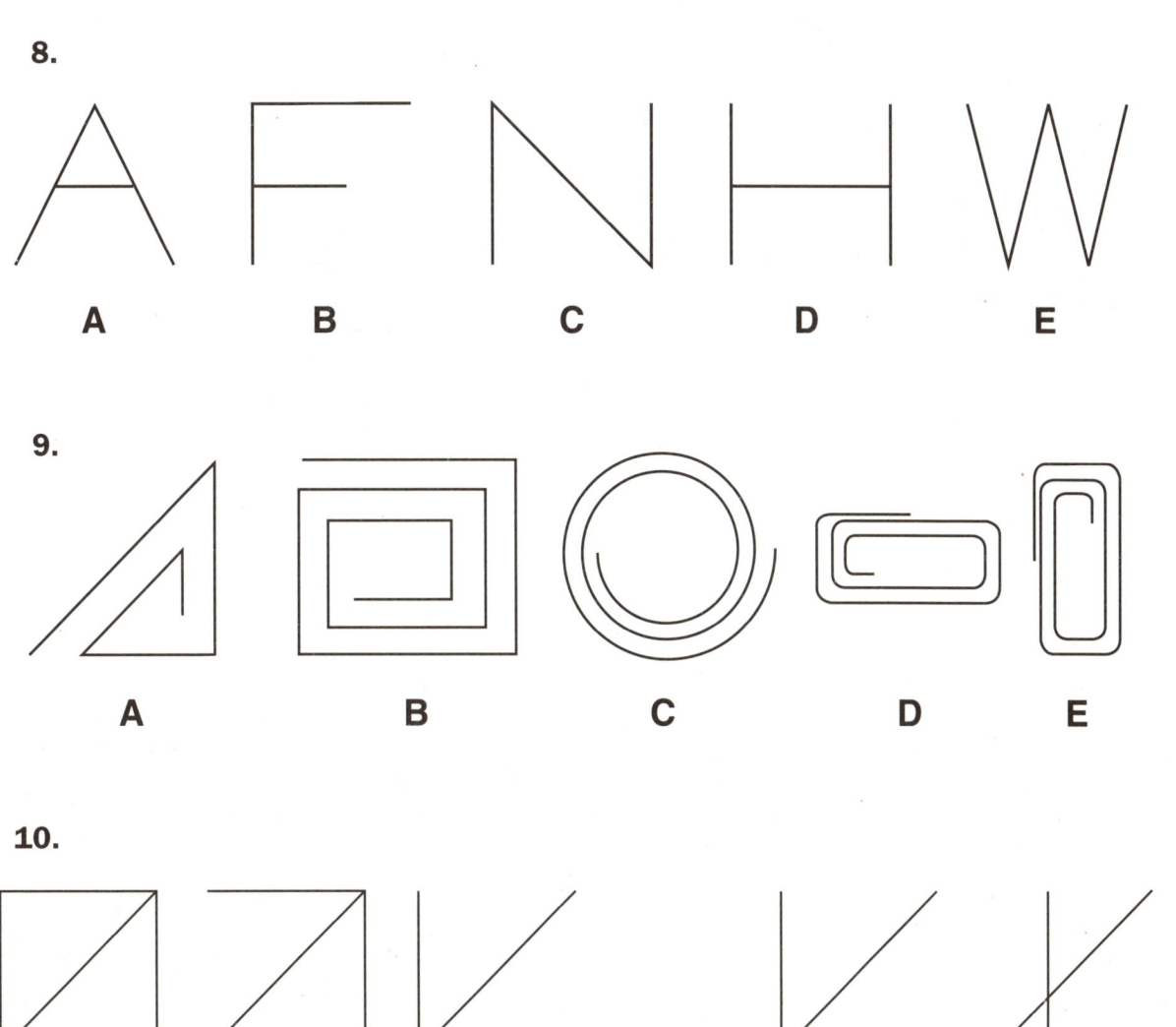

8. A B C D E

9. A B C D E

10. A B C D E

Answers on page 127

ZONE 5

OBSTACLE 2 Which arrangement is missing from these sequences?

11.

    A   B   C   D   E

12.

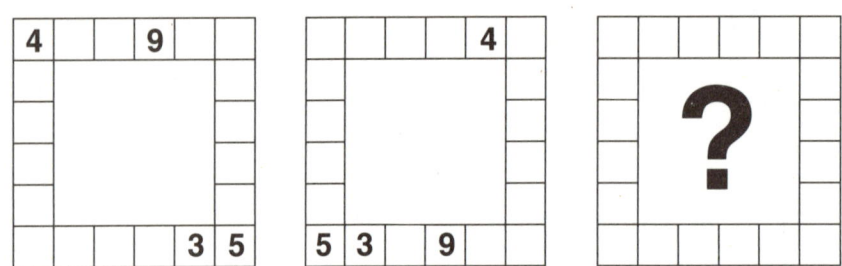 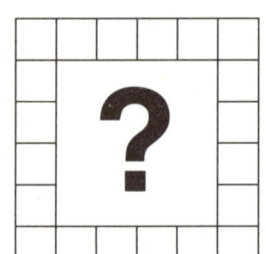 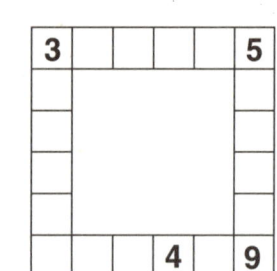

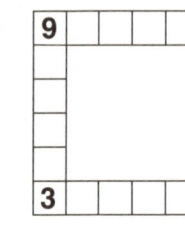 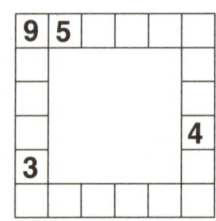 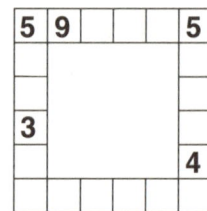

    A   B   C   D   E

Answers on page 127

13.

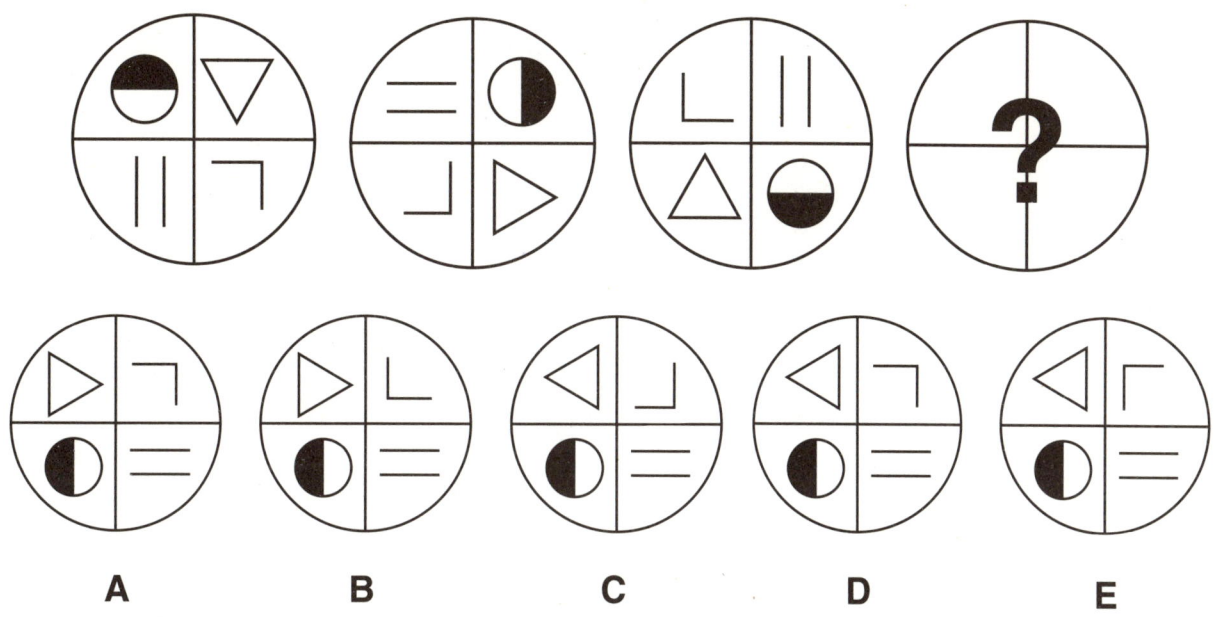

14.

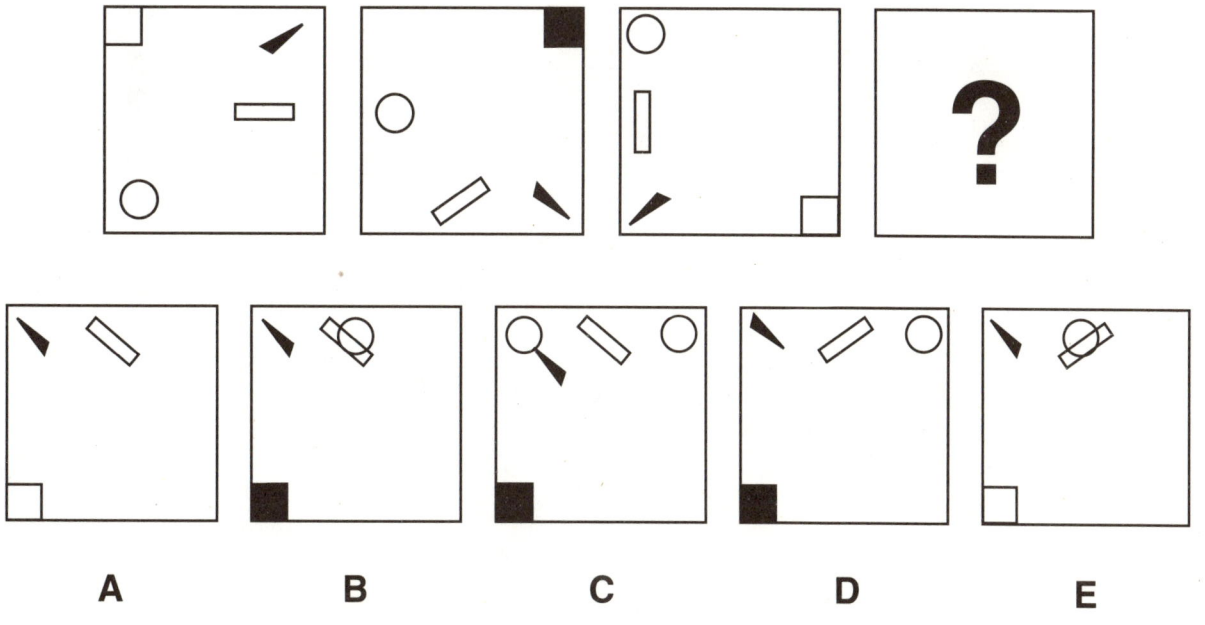

Answers on page 127

ZONE 5

THE SPATIAL LOGIC DODGE

15.

16.

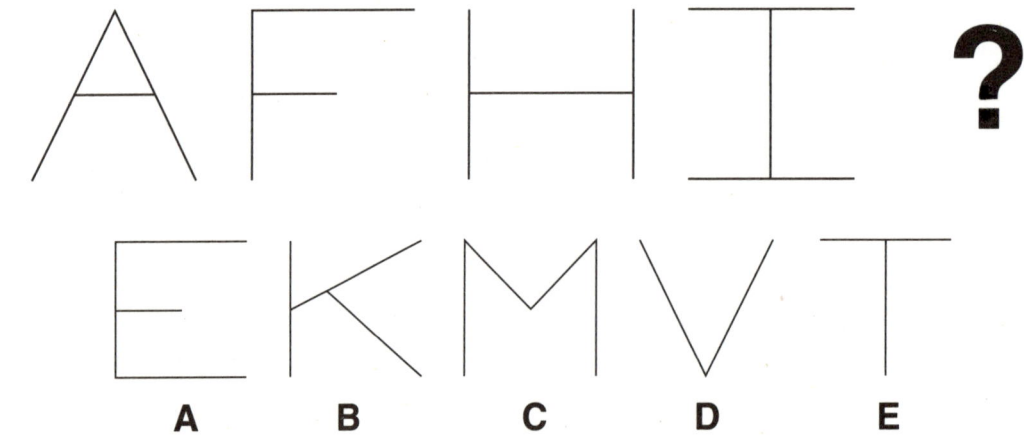

112 Answers on page 127

17.

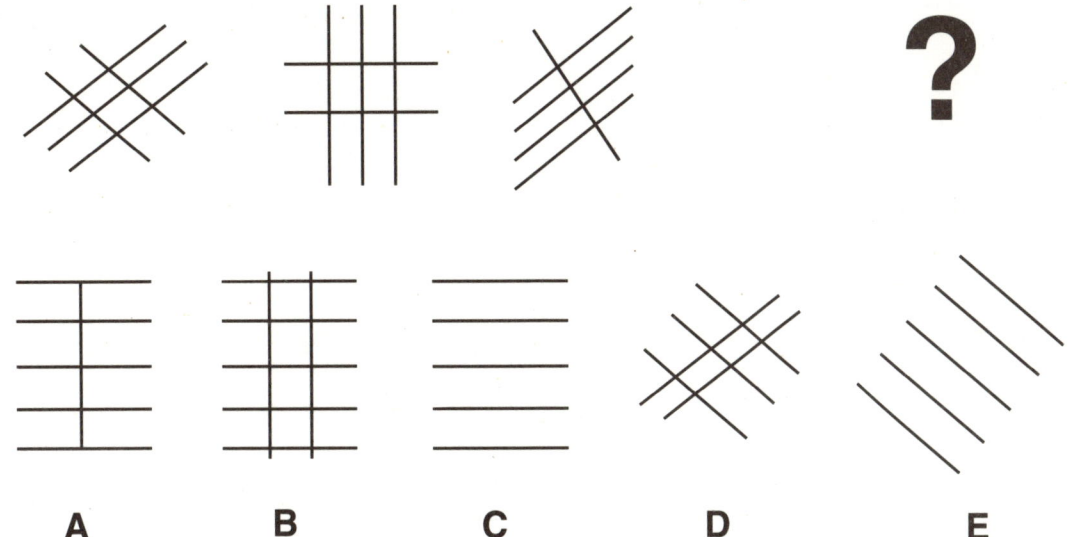

18.

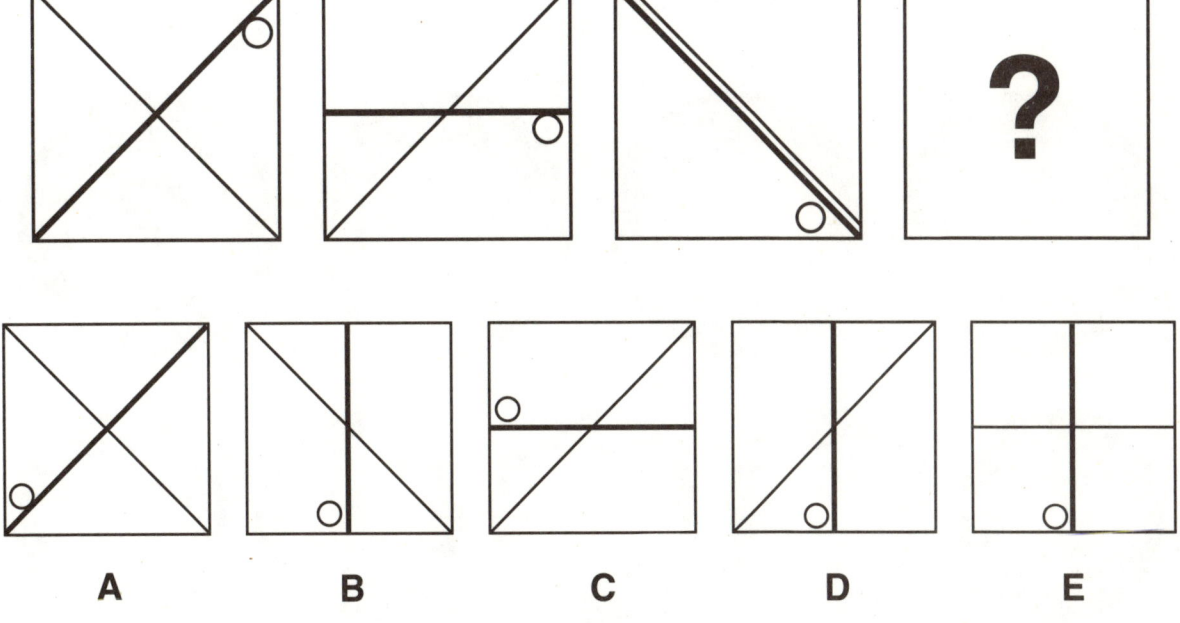

ZONE 5

19.

20.

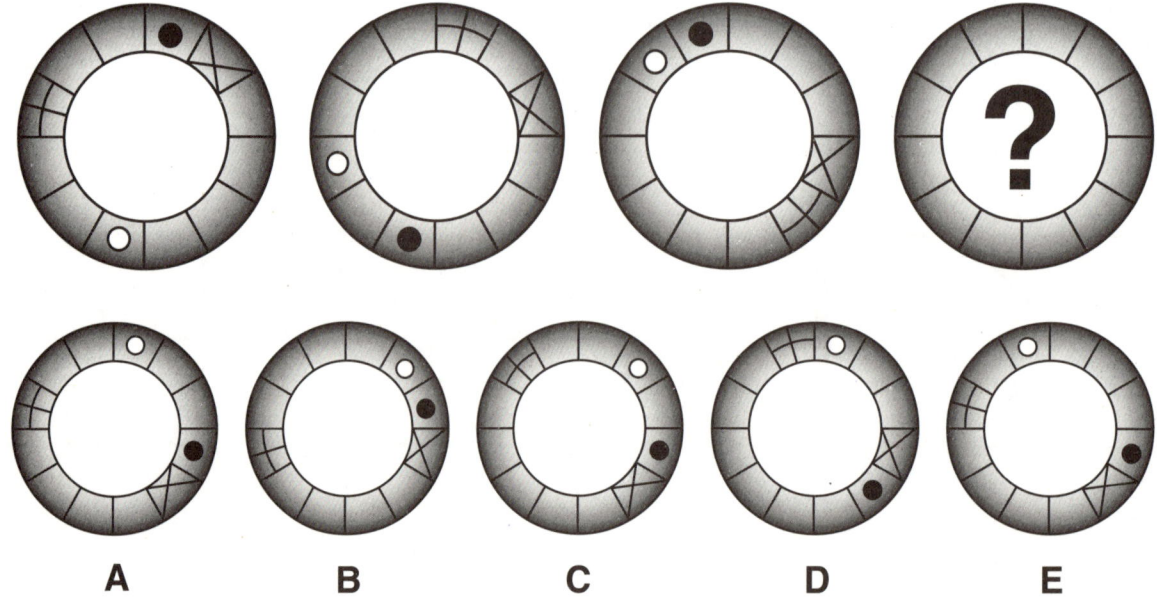

114 Answers on page 127

21.

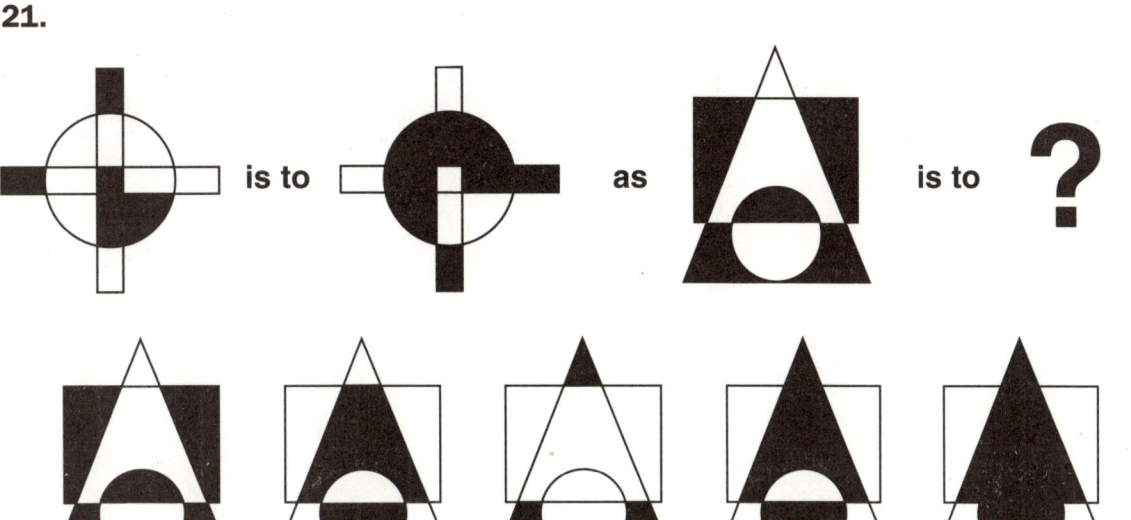

22.

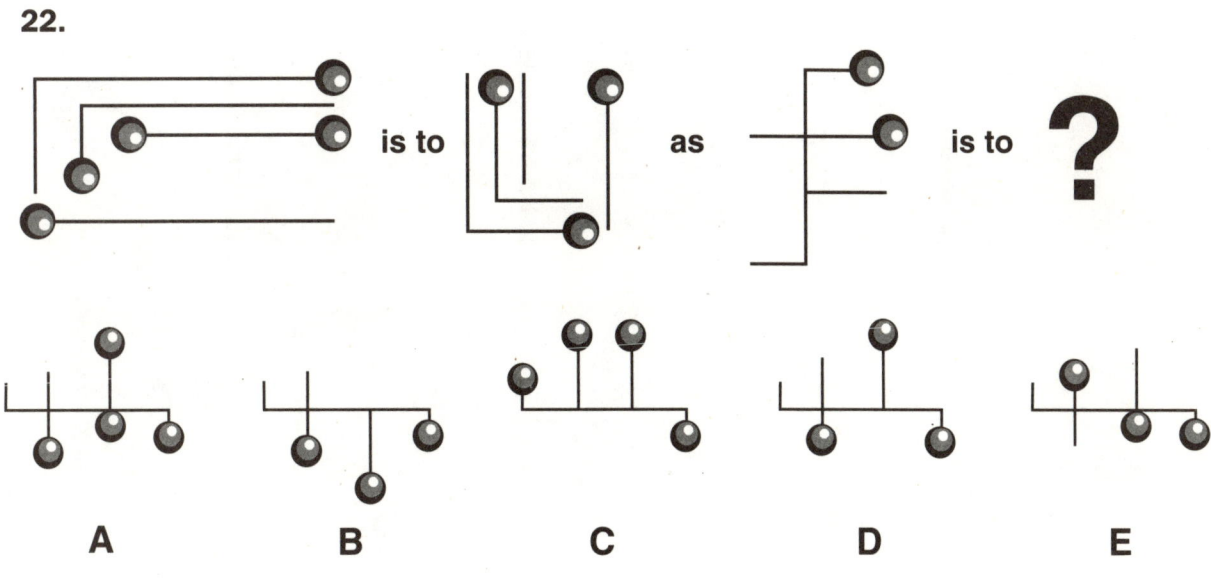

ZONE 5

23.

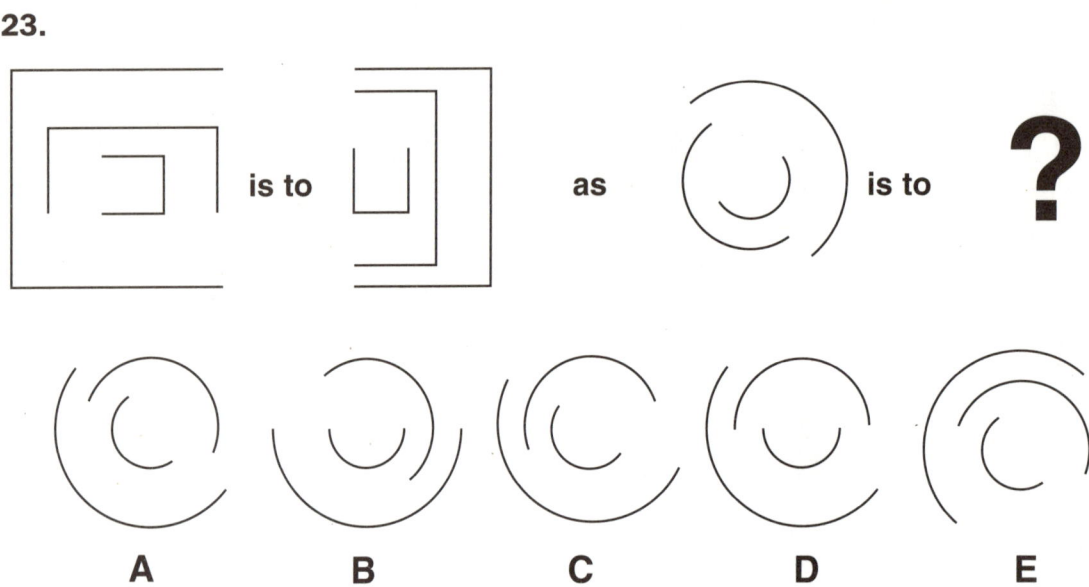

24.

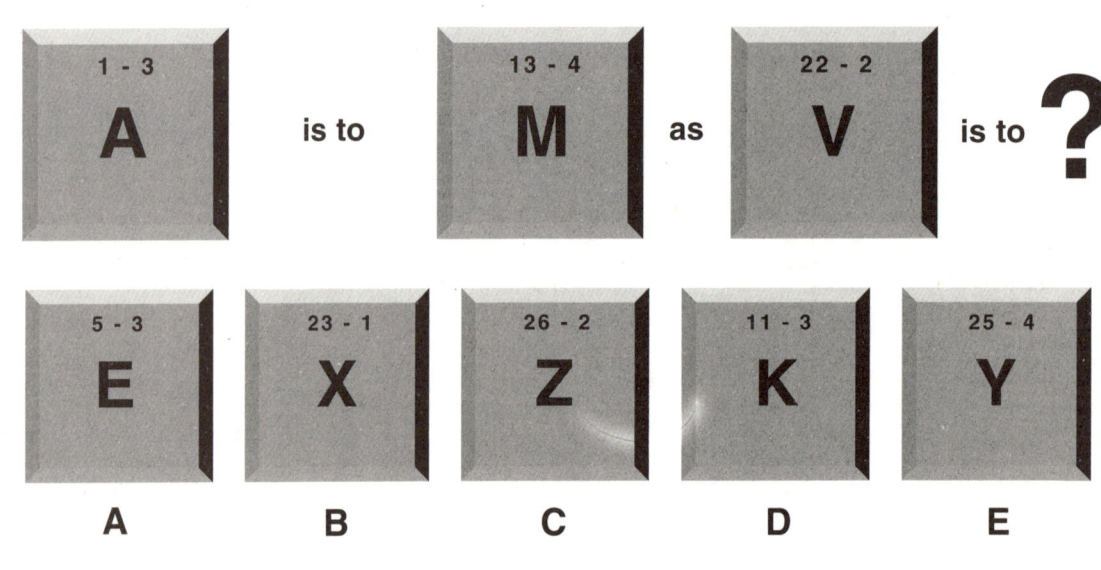

116 Answers on page 127

25.

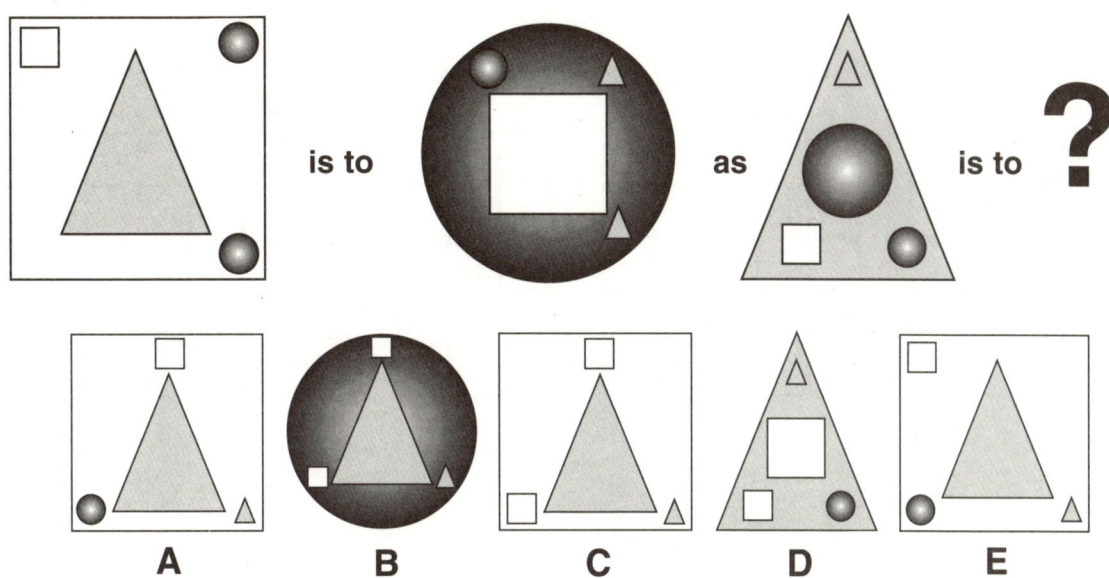

OBSTACLE 3 These are all mirror image problems. One of the 4 given images has an error on it.

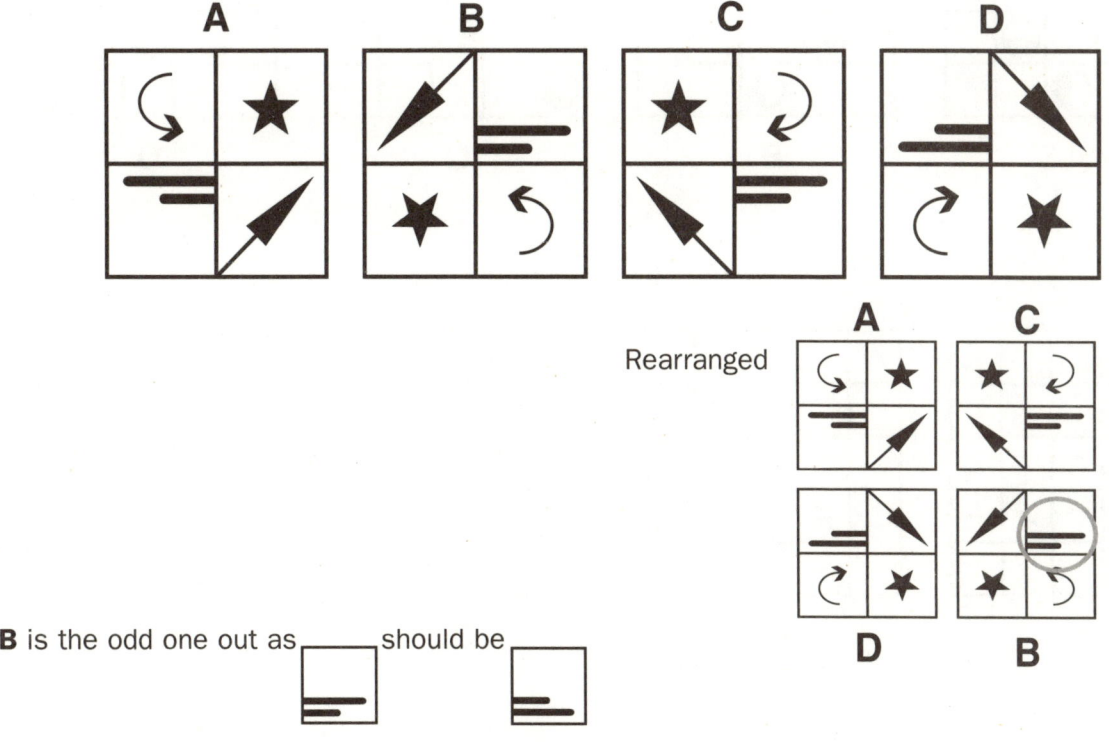

B is the odd one out as [ ] should be [ ]

ZONE 5

Each one of the next five puzzles is a mirror image problem. Which of A, B, C or D is the odd one out?

26.

A

B

C

D

27.

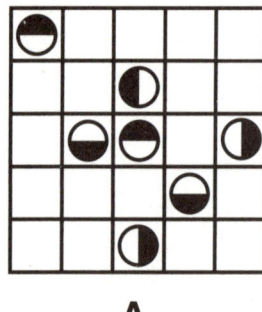
A

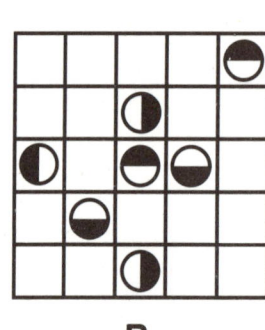
B

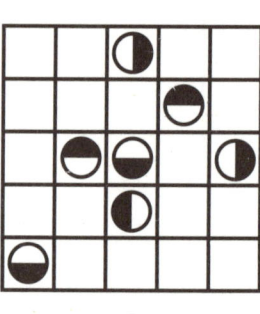
C

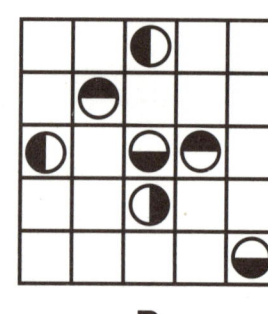
D

28.

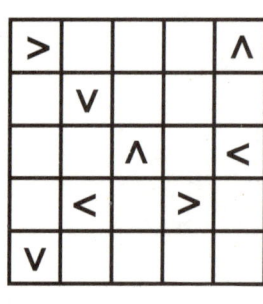
A

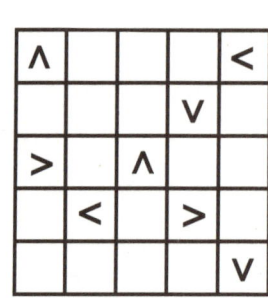
B

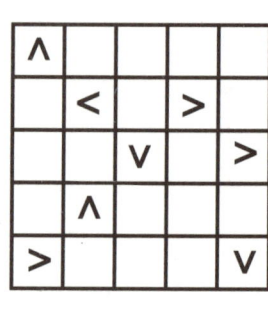
C

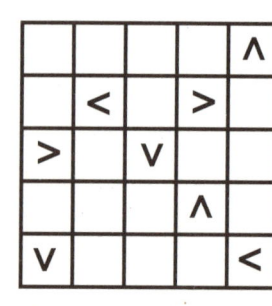
D

Answers on page 127

29.

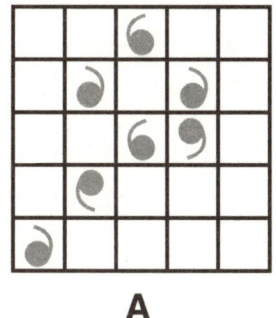
A

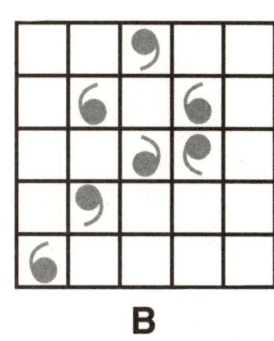
B

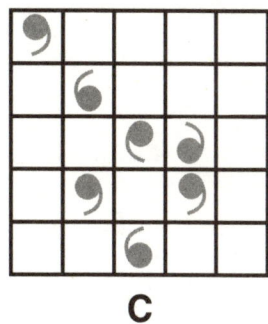
C

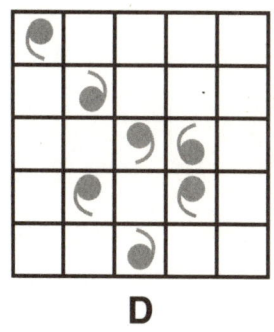
D

30.

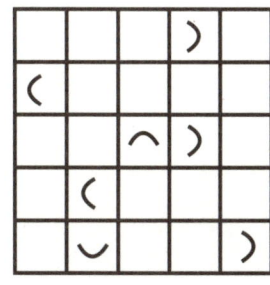
A

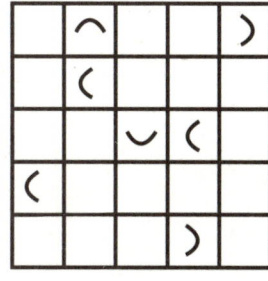
B

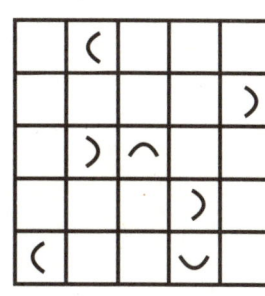
C

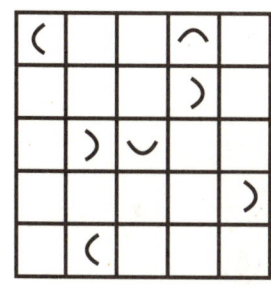
D

OBSTACLE 4 No sign is used on more than one side of the box. Which of these is not a view of the same box?

31.

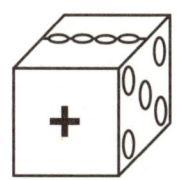
A

B

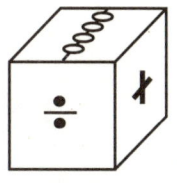
C

D

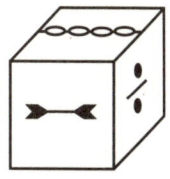
E

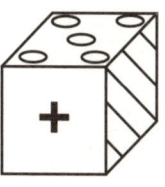
F

ZONE 5

THE SPATIAL LOGIC DODGE

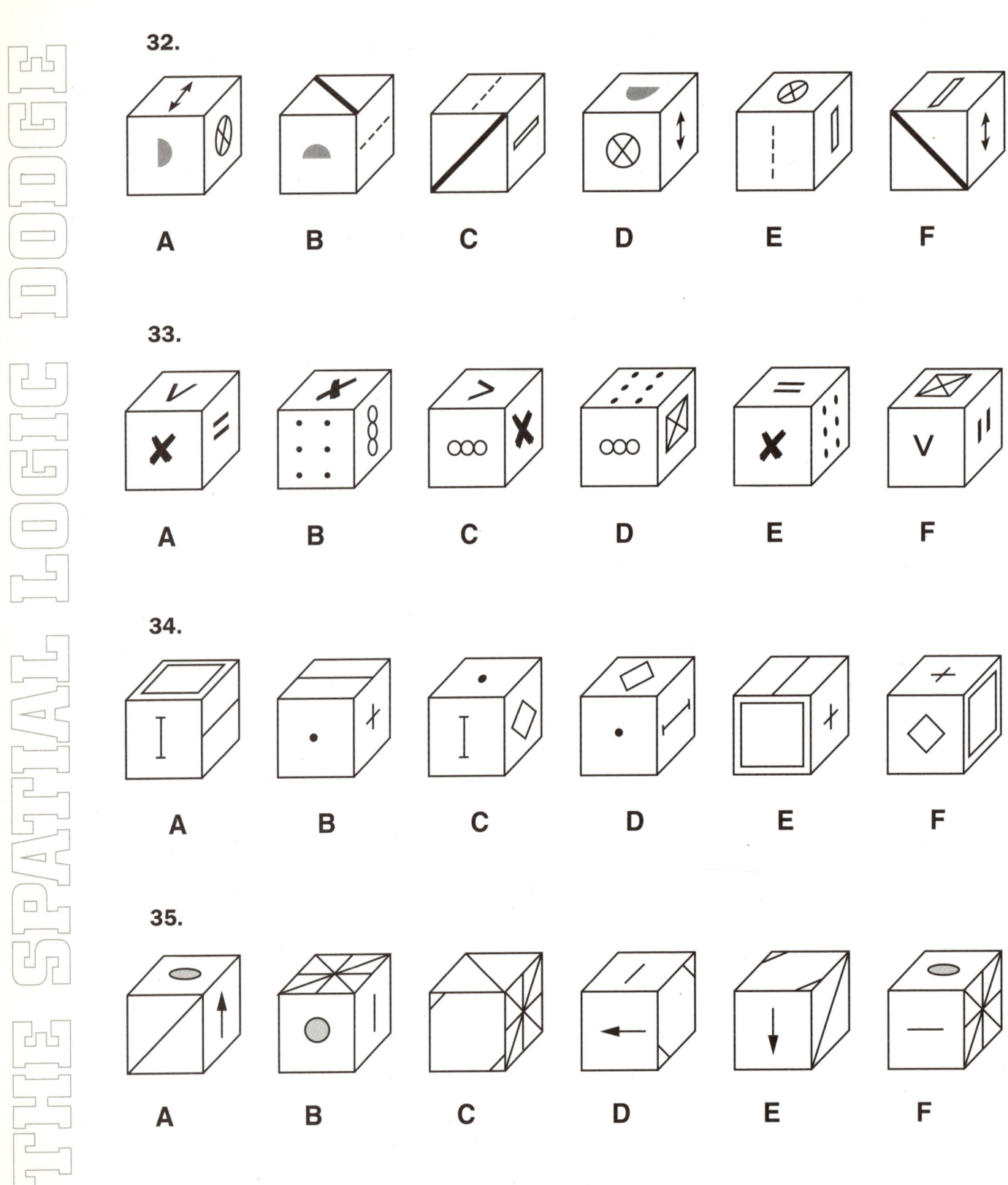

120 Answers on page 127

ZONE 5

OBSTACLE 5 Which of these boxes can be made from the template? No sign is repeated on more than one side of the box.

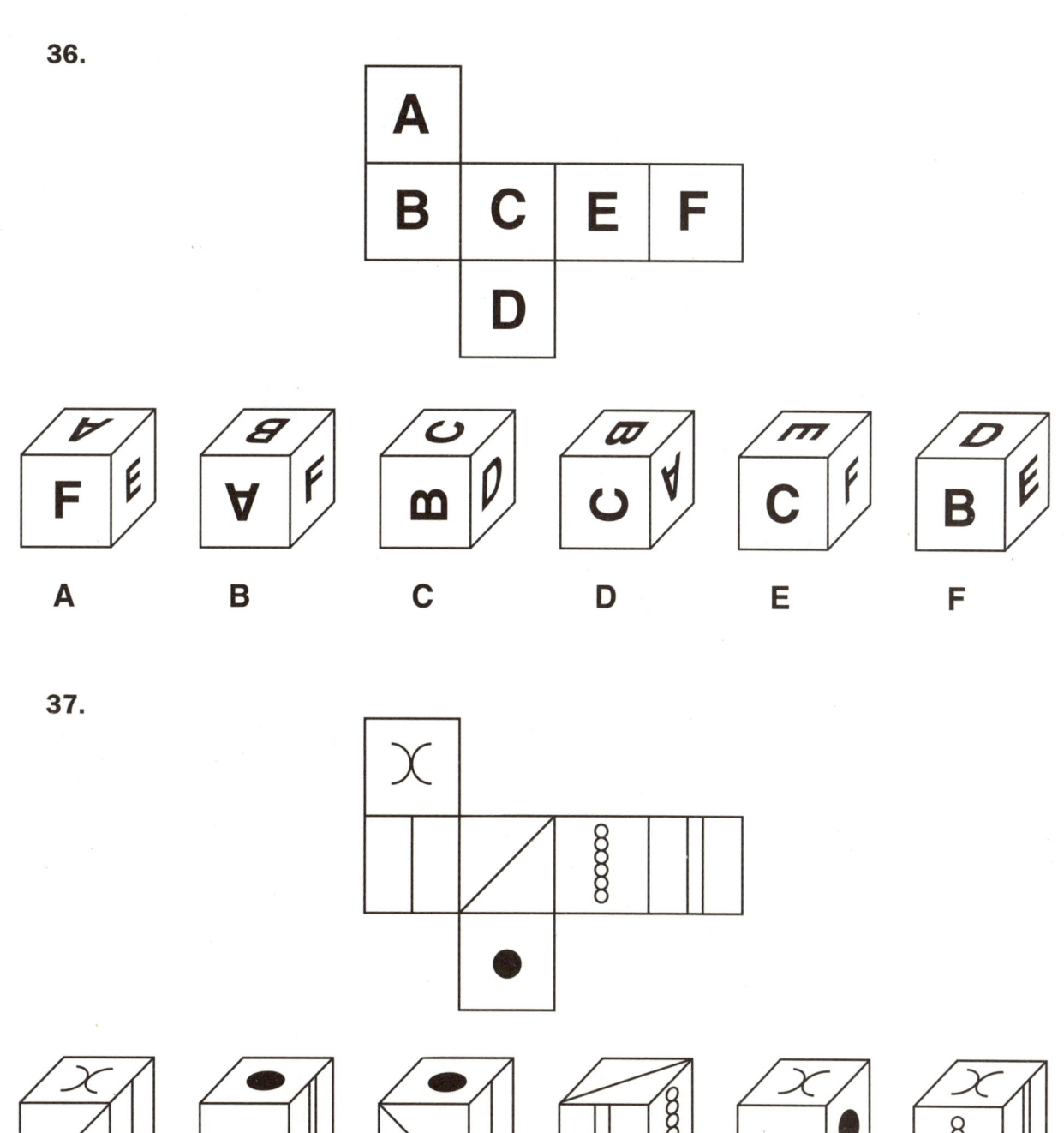

36.

37.

Answers on page 127

THE SPATIAL LOGIC DODGE

ZONE 5

THE SPATIAL LOGIC DODGE

38.

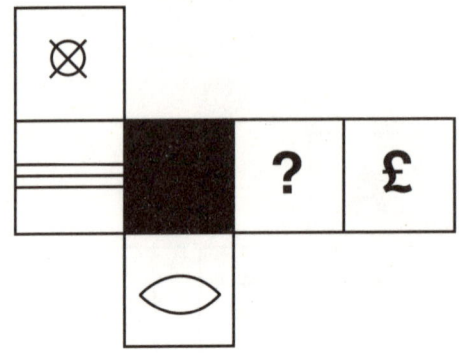

 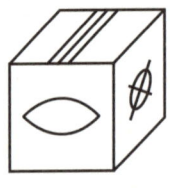    

A   B   C   D   E   F

39.

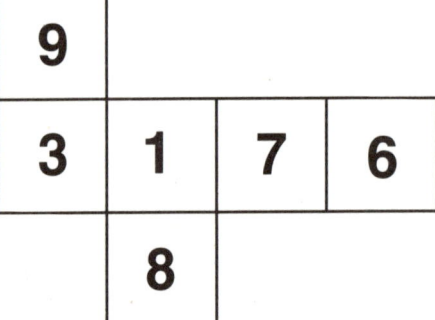

A   B   C   D   E   F

Answers on page 127

ZONE 5

THE SPATIAL LOGIC DODGE

40.

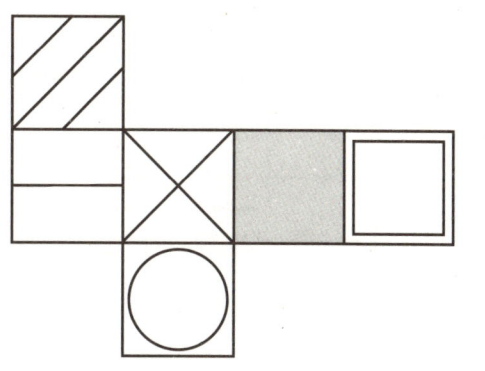

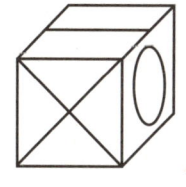  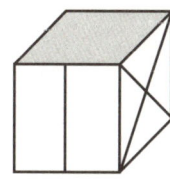 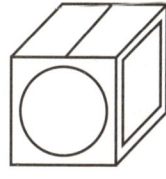 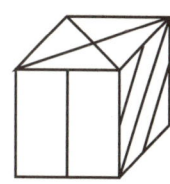 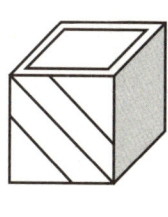

A   B   C   D   E   F

OBSTACLE 6 Can you determine which shape has not been used in these questions?

41.

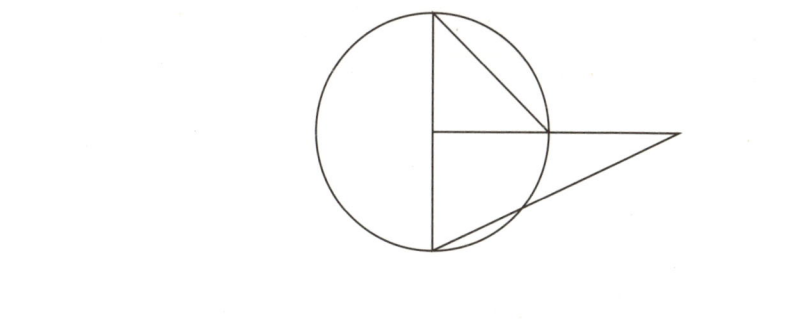

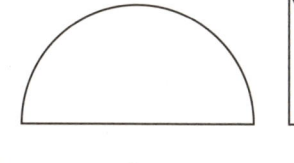 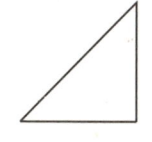 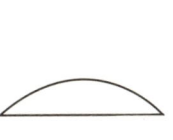 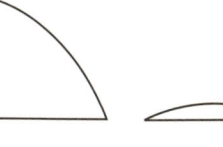 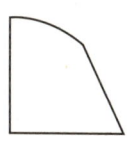

A   B   C   D   E   F   G

Answers on pages 127 & 128

ZONE 5

THE SPATIAL LOGIC DODGE

42.

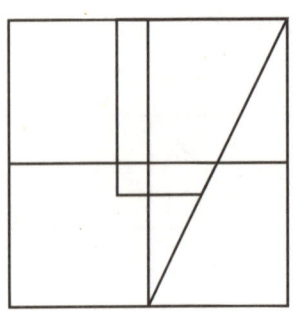

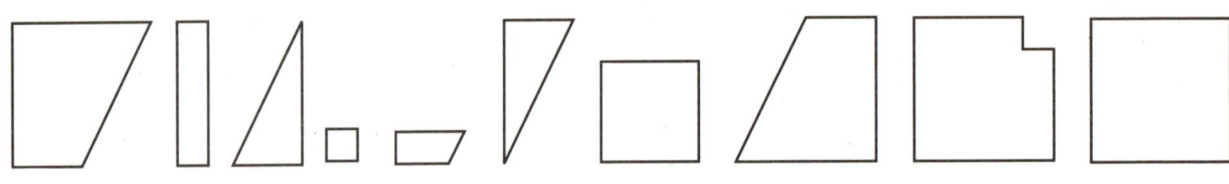

A   B   C   D   E   F   G   H   I   J

43.

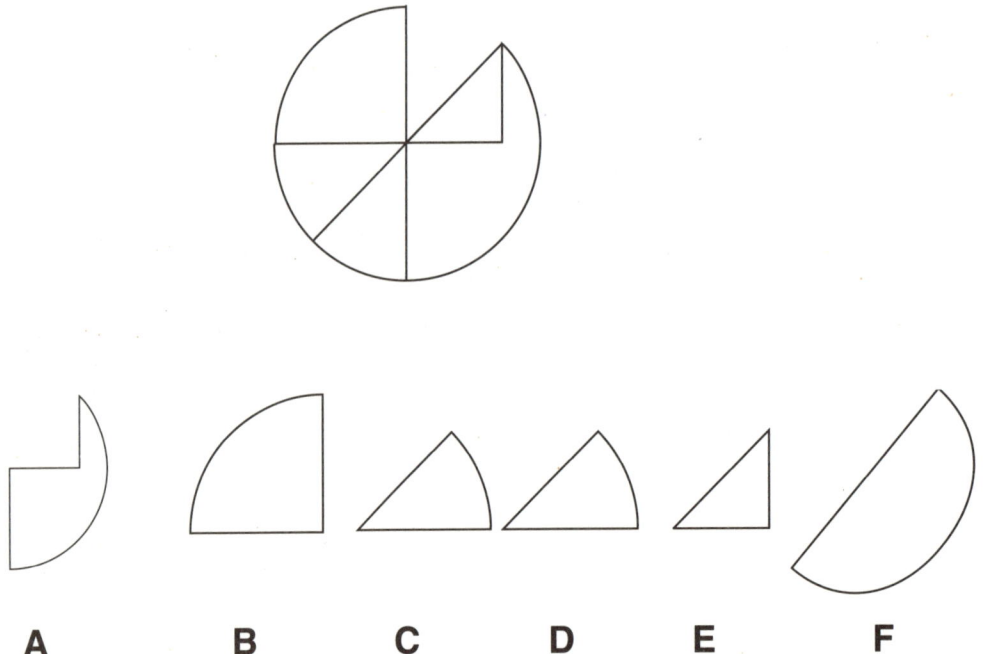

A   B   C   D   E   F

Answers on page 128

124

ZONE 5

THE SPATIAL LOGIC DODGE

OBSTACLE 7   In the puzzles below, which shape should replace the question mark?

44.

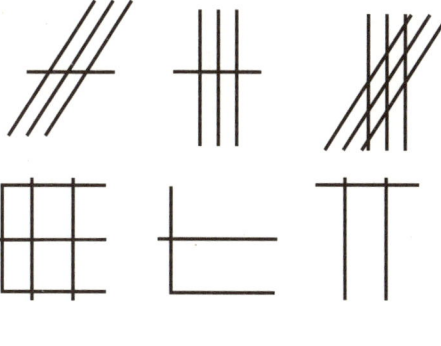
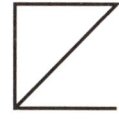

A   B   C   D   E

45.

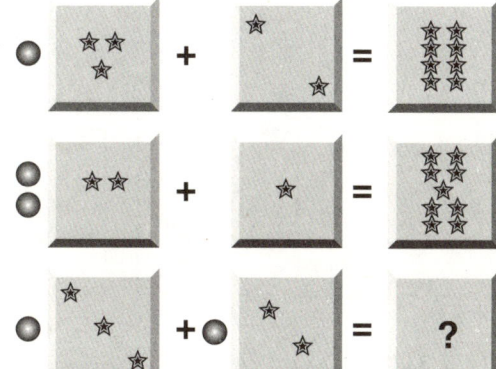

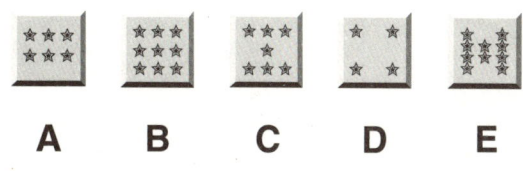

A   B   C   D   E

OBSTACLE 8   Which of the shapes – A, B, C, D or E – cannot be made from the dots if a line is drawn through all of the dots at least once?

46.

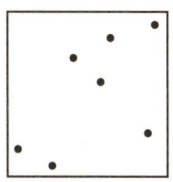  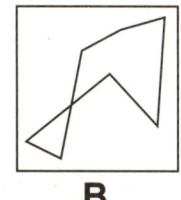   

        A   B   C   D   E

Answers on page 128

ZONE 5

47.

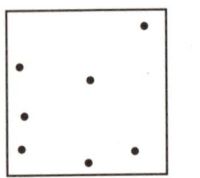 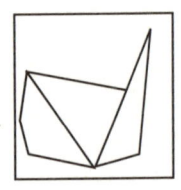   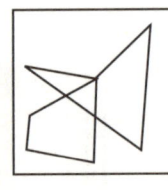 

A B C D E

48.

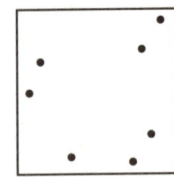  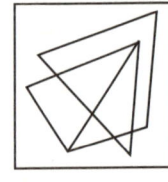 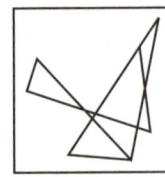 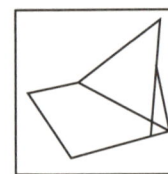 

A B C D E

49.

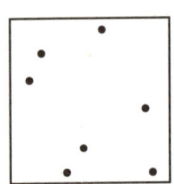 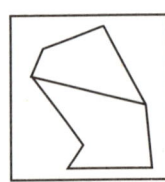 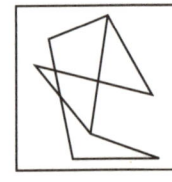 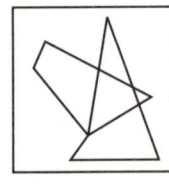 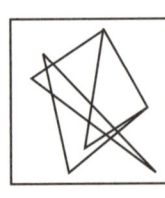 

A B C D E

50.

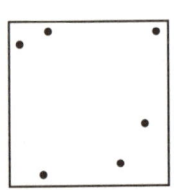 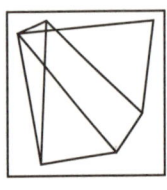  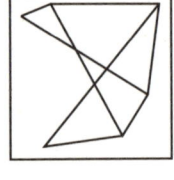  

A B C D E

Answers on page 128

ZONE 5

ANSWERS

OBSTACLE 1

1. C. Others rotate into the same shape.
2. D. A & E and B & C form opposite pairs.
3. C. Others are Roman numerals rotated 90° anti- (counter) clockwise.
4. D. Others rotate into the same shape.
5. E. Others rotate into the same shape.
6. A. Others rotate into the same shape.
7. B. A & D and C & E form opposite pairs.
8. E. It contains four lines; the others have only three.
9. D. The pattern inside does not go clockwise.
10. E. The others are made of two shapes.

OBSTACLE 2

11. A. Binary system, start at 5 and add 3 each time. You can also find the answer by treating the images as a negative and mirror-imaging them.
12. B. Numbers rotate clockwise by the number given.
13. E. The figures rotate one sector at a time.
14. B. Shapes rotate in sequence.
15. A. Shapes rotate in sequence.
16. B. All use three lines.
17. C. Rotates and lines are subtracted from one and added to the other.
18. D. Rotating shapes.
19. D. Small circles move left to right and bottom to top.
20. A. Each shape rotates in a set sequence.
21. D. Matched opposite pairs.
22. A. Whole figure rotates 90° anti- (counter) clockwise and circles are reversed at end of lines.
23. C. Rotations in sequence.
24. D. First number is alpha-numeric position (eg, A=1).
25. A. Square becomes circle, triangle becomes square, circle becomes triangle.

OBSTACLE 3

26. D.
27. B.
28. C.
29. A.
30. A.

OBSTACLE 4

31. D.
32. B.
33. B.
34. E.
35. C.

OBSTACLE 5

36. C.
37. F.
38. E.
39. A.
40. F.

ZONE 5

OBSTACLE 6
41. E.
42. G.
43. F.

OBSTACLE 7
44. E. Duplicated lines on first two of each row are deleted in third figure.
45. E. • = (numbers of stars x 2) + numbers of stars = number of stars in column 3.

OBSTACLE 8
46. E.
47. A.
48. D.
49. E.
50. B.

Scoring System

The Spatial Logic Assessment

If you have done well in this section you probably have a well-organized and structured mind. Just the sort the Mind Army needs.

Promotion Criteria (See page 21):

Under 20	Busted one rank.
21 - 30	No promotion.
31 - 40	Promoted one rank.
41+	Promoted two ranks.

Age Bonus Points

Age in Years	10	10.5	11	11.5	12	12.5	13	13.5	14	14.5	15	15.5
Bonus Points	10	10	9	8	7	6	6	5	4	3	2	1